Miłego
Toaemia
się
i Amiotkam

Angel Thinking

A Guidebook into the World of Oneness and Love

Lorelei A. Hill

Angel Thinking

Copyright © 2012 by Lorelei A. Hill.

All rights reserved. No part of this book may be used or reproduced by any means, graphic, electronic, or mechanical, including photocopying, recording, taping or by any information storage retrieval system without the written permission of the publisher except in the case of brief quotations embodied in critical articles and reviews.

ISBN: 978-1-4525-6333-6 (sc)
ISBN: 978-1-4525-6334-3 (e)

Library of Congress Control Number: 2012921835

Balboa Press books may be ordered through booksellers or by contacting:

Balboa Press
A Division of Hay House
1663 Liberty Drive
Bloomington, IN 47403
www.balboapress.com
1-(877) 407-4847

Because of the dynamic nature of the Internet, any web addresses or links contained in this book may have changed since publication and may no longer be valid. The views expressed in this work are solely those of the author and do not necessarily reflect the views of the publisher, and the publisher hereby disclaims any responsibility for them.

The author of this book does not dispense medical advice or prescribe the use of any technique as a form of treatment for physical, emotional, or medical problems without the advice of a physician, either directly or indirectly. The intent of the author is only to offer information of a general nature to help you in your quest for emotional and spiritual well-being. In the event you use any of the information in this book for yourself, which is your constitutional right, the author and the publisher assume no responsibility for your actions.

Any people depicted in stock imagery provided by Thinkstock are models, and such images are being used for illustrative purposes only.
Certain stock imagery © Thinkstock.

Printed in the United States of America

Balboa Press rev. date: 11/27/12

Dear Earth Angel,

    I was five years old when I rode my tricycle off of my father's dock. The weight of the bike pulled me to the bottom of the deep lake. Instead of being scared, calm overtook me as I submerged. In that instant I knew I was completely safe. "We are with you." The angels sang as they swam in ribbons of color towards me. Their utter love filled me with peace. It felt as though I had gone home. Having seen my fall, my quick acting cousin dove into the water and pulled me to the shore, thus ending my first known human encounter with my angels.

    In this book you will find many paths for connecting with your own angels. Whether this is your first angel encounter or you have been working with angels all your life, these fun and simple exercises will help you and your children to become better acquainted with fifteen of my favorite archangels. Follow your intuition as you follow your heart along this journey. Angels are with you each and every minute. Learn how to hear your angels' whisper, feel their love, and discover the signs that say, "We are with you, Earth Angel."

Love and gratitude,
Lorelei

PREFACE

Why Angels?

ON THE EVENING OF my daughter's eighth birthday, she came to me in tears.

"Mommy," she said, "Chloe is gone."

Chloe is what many people would call an imaginary friend. This was a sad moment. Who would Katie turn to when in need of quiet reassurance or gentle comfort in the night? Who would Katie laugh with when friends could not be near? Chloe is more than just an imaginary friend. She is my daughter's guardian angel.

As a primary schoolteacher, I have long believed that young children can see a world that adults cannot. So I was not surprised when Katie told me that a young girl sat by her bedside each night. Nor was I surprised when she told me how Chloe had appeared to her on the schoolyard whenever she felt frightened by a bully or shunned by her circle of friends.

My ten-year-old son Riley often speaks of the two male angels who, standing in his doorway, watch over him while he sleeps. And why shouldn't he? As a young girl, I myself experienced frequent visits from guardian angels. I also remember the sadness I felt when my visitors seemed nowhere to be found.

Shortly after my eighteenth birthday, like a floodgate opening, a visit from a recently deceased friend brought memories of my spirit friends soaring back. Shawn's awakening in me was followed by a series of visits from my grandfather's spirit. It was at that time, in my twenties, when I realized what I had seen as a child was more than just my imagination. So when Katie announced that Chloe had left her side, it only seemed right that I turn to my angel guides for help.

"Thank you always for your loving guidance," I said. "Please, dearest angels, help me to find a way to keep you alive in the hearts and minds of my son and daughter, and all children of the world. I give myself to you for the greatest good."

Almost immediately a voice told me to find a sketchbook and "let your hand simply draw." The result is the collection of original drawings included at the end of each chapter alongside my good friend Antje's artistic interpretation of our combined visions.

I hadn't realized at the time that these drawings were only the beginning of the inspiration my heavenly guides were about to send. As I sketched, I began to hear whispers all around me. They were subtle, soft, and oh so loving! Soon I could see angelic signs almost everywhere I went. With each passing day, a new angel made himself known to me.

This book is the result of these divine communications. Within its pages, you will read the angels' words of wisdom and guidance to me. Intended to be a fun and helpful means of reconnecting with your angels, *Angel Thinking* also contains historical information relating to fifteen prominent archangels and their choirs. As each chapter addresses a new archangel, you will learn the meaning of the angel's name, its place in heaven, and why it is present in your life.

The angels directed me to write *Angel Thinking* as a guidebook into their world of oneness and love. While it is not my intention to breach personal religious points of view, some readers may find pieces of information passed down to me by the angels and contained within the pages of this text to be outside their formal belief systems. Remembering that angels are referenced in every faith, my advice for parents and teachers is to read the angels' messages on your own or with a partner. Only then can you decide how much or how little you intend to share with your children.

Please approach this reading with an open heart and an open mind, all the while celebrating the renewed connection with your spiritual guides. I wish you a truly angelic journey!

DEDICATION

For
Riley, Katie, and Mike - Angels of my heart,
Yvonne and Antje - soul sisters,
And all the earth angels who pick up this book.

ABOUT THE AUTHOR

In the quiet of her room, Mary, Queen of Angels appeared. Sitting on the edge of the bed, a simple nod and smile was all she gave. It was all that was necessary to feel her love. Lorelei didn't need to ask her name, she already knew. At a very young age Lorelei Hill had begun receiving messages from her angel guides.

On the morning of her first open-heart surgery, Archangel Azrael filled her hospital room with light and love. From within the light, Lorelei received the reassuring message that she was safe. She went into surgery calm and confident, knowing she would survive.

Despite doctor's warnings about what she couldn't do, Lorelei has lived her life the way she intended. Earning an Honors Degree in Reformation and Religious History along with a B.Ed. from Queen's University, she took her talents abroad to write and teach.

Lorelei's passion for life and steadfast faith is an inspirational story of endurance. Born in 1963 with a rare, often fatal heart disorder, she refused to let her condition define her. Despite numerous surgeries, Lorelei lived her life with determination and courage. On March 10, 2012, she had the distinction of becoming the second and oldest Fontan patient in Canada to survive heart transplant.

Lorelei is a speaker, educator and adviser to congenital children and their families. She also spends her days writing and creating pastel paintings depicting how she 'sees' her angels. ***Angel Thinking*** is the culmination of sacred times in Lorelei's life when angels have come to guide her.

CONTENTS

Preface vii
Dedication ix
About the Author xi
Foreword xv
Angel Guides xvii
Chapter 1: Do Angels Care about Us? And Why Are They
    So Important to Our Personal Lives? 1
Chapter 2: Archangel Ariel 3
Chapter 3: Archangel Azrael 15
Chapter 4: Archangel Chamuel 27
Chapter 5: Archangel Gabriel 37
Chapter 6: Archangel Haniel 47
Chapter 7: Archangel Jeremiel 55
Chapter 8: Archangel Jophiel 65
Chapter 9: Archangel Metatron 73
Chapter 10: Archangel Michael 83
Chapter 11: Archangel Raphael 93
Chapter 12: Archangel Raguel 103
Chapter 13: Archangel Raziel 113
Chapter 14: Archangel Sandalphon 123
Chapter 15: Archangel Uriel 133
Chapter 16: Archangel Zadkiel 143
Chapter 17: A Final Word 151
Appendix: 153
Balloon Breathing 155
Calling all Angels 157
Bibliography 159

FOREWORD

"I tell you the truth, anyone who will not receive the kingdom of God like a little child will never enter it." Luke 18:17

ANGELS! WHO AMONG US has never thought about these heavenly beings? Children seem to have an especially close connection to them. When asked they often describe them as bright, tall, elegant or winged persons. My daughter says, "You can feel angels but you can't see them."

All my life I was intrigued by the idea of angels. As a child I only needed to close my eyes to see a dance of colors. They came in lines and shapes and flashes. In fever dreams they became bold and so big that they scared me. Other times they were just little sparks that made me laugh. I didn't know what the colors meant, but I certainly didn't connect them to angels.

Butterflies landed on my hand or in my hair, cats followed me down the street, and sheep would leave their flock to greet me at the fence when my family and I were on our Sunday walk. My parents praised my close and intuitive relationship to animals and often silently wondered – but nobody perceived any spiritual guidance there.

Like most sensitive children, I saw things my family and friends didn't notice. I didn't quite understand my vivid and foreboding dreams, or my photogenic memory, to be a gift. Not wanting to be perceived as weird, I learned not to talk about such things. Trying to be normal and fit in, I ignored my intuitive wisdom and connection to the otherworld until after years of studying, I seemed to have lost it completely. Luckily, as Marianne Williamson[1] said, "The world we knew as children is still buried within our minds."

---

1 Williamson, Marianne, A Return to Love, HarperCollins Publishers, New York, New York, 1992, p. xxiv

When years later, I met my good friend and author Lorelei Hill many of our conversations led to angels. She seemed to know a lot about the heavenly beings who had always intrigued me. Neither of us could relate to the renaissance images of fat little baby-like beings with wings. I realized then that I was not the only person full of questions. After many nudges from humans and angels alike, Lorelei began to write the book you are holding in your hands right now. ***Angel Thinking*** was born.

Challenging as it was, it has been an honor and a blessing to illustrate this wonderful and easy-to-read book. Before painting the fifteen archangels, I spent various amounts of time with each individual angel, meditating and allowing them to guide my hand.

Some paintings came fast and easy and often agreed with the original sketches I got from Lorelei. Others requested more of my time and came with a lesson I had to learn first before I understood how each angel wanted to be seen. It was a miraculous journey and I am pleased to say that it continues. As you complete the exercises in this book, you too will come to know the angels in your own personal way.

During our work with the angels in the creation of this book, a very special miracle happened. Lorelei received a long awaited new heart!

I'd like to invite you to read ***Angel Thinking*** with an open-mind and to allow yourself to get involved with the heavenly beings. The archangels are loving, supportive guides who will make your life easier and more enjoyable too.

I personally got a new understanding of their guidance and love and I can sense their presence in many ways. I still see them in colors when I close my eyes, I see them in butterflies dancing along my path, in clouds painted into the sky and in messages written on billboards or whispered into my ears.

As Lorelei and I did, you will have your own unique way of seeing and experiencing the angels. In all your journeys, may you be surrounded in every way by angelic protection, love and support.

ANGEL GUIDES

Angelic Choirs

Thinking of winged singers? Can you hear their heavenly voices rise in song? Have *you* ever heard the angels sing? If you said no, you are not alone.

No Sound

The faithful believe angels profess love to God, Yahweh, The Divine Universe, I Am, and The One when gathered in song. Known by many names, in angel society these entities are all the same.

Great and Wondrous

Though few people admit to hearing angels sing, angelic choirs are still held to be the most beautiful music-makers in heaven. As one, on this earth, we humans create our own choirs of joy and praise.

Everywhere

Angels may seem quiet, but that doesn't stop them from serving you. Surrounding The Divine Universe, your angels are always revealing your true Goodness to the world.

Like Angels

Your body conceals what is inside of you just as the angels shelter I Am. Acts of kindness and expression of talent are the Good in you that your body cannot hide. You, earth angel, are a member of angel society.

Go the Distance

Your job is to play like heaven is on earth. Before long, you'll see that heaven *is* on earth.

Unconditional

You have at least one guardian angel, and it is impossible to count the choirs and legions of angels with you at all times. There is, after all, one very special angel who does that for us. Archangel Azrael is his name.

Incumbent

Like angelic parents, Azrael and the other archangels guide you each day.

Dependent

The archangels love you just as your mother, father, or others who care for you. Most notably, their job is to teach choirs, bands, and legions of angels how to best guide for you.

Enter Angel Society

Begin your most incredible journey. Witness true wonders of the world. Simply turn the page, meet your heavenly guides, and welcome the inspiration they bring you.

Share Love

Angels are divine spirits who exist to reveal their love. Uncovering *your* hidden talents, they reveal God's grace. By assisting you in acts of kindness, angels show their love in the eyes of others. Their message to you is simple. Share love.

We are from God. We are caregivers of the earth. We are one.

CHAPTER 1

Do Angels Care about Us? And Why Are They So Important to Our Personal Lives?

ANGELS ARE WITH US every minute of every day. They bring us gifts from the spirit world. They are here to help us remember who we are and why we are on this earth. Just look around, and you will see a sign that an angel is near. It could be a butterfly fluttering past your nose, or a perfect bird's feather lying in the grass. An angel can ring a chime or cast a faintly colored light. An angel can even send you feelings of happiness or a warm blanket hug. Angels come to us in many ways. Our only job is to trust they are near.

This can sometimes be difficult since angels are heavenly beings not human beings. It may sound strange, but angels don't actually have human qualities. They are neither male nor female and are never afraid or angry. Angels are patient, kind, and loving. They show themselves to humans in many forms. When we feel there is an angel present but can't see one, it helps to think of the angel as having a human appearance. An angel that I might describe as a young lady could appear to you as a young boy or an older man. Yours might even look like a spark of light, a dragonfly, or a wild cat! A tiny black dog or a hummingbird! And guess what? We would both be right!

Those who play like the angels will begin to talk, act, and think like them. What better way for us to spot our heavenly guides? The truth is that angels are everywhere. So the next time you think an angel might be near, strap on your imagination and quiet the voice inside your head that says, "If you can't see it, it ain't there."

Come on! Let's go find your angels!

CHAPTER 2

Archangel Ariel

The Lion of God

Archangel Ariel whispers to you, "Grab your sketchbook and pencil. Come follow me! Walk lightly through the forest. What do you see? Notice the gifts Mother Earth hides in front of your eyes. Look with your heart. Listen with your soul!"

FOR THE ANGEL so closely connected to the natural world, Archangel Ariel came to me in a very strange place. During a hospital stay, I was asked to lie on a hard narrow bed. The hospital technicians pulled straps around me so I would be perfectly still while a large MRI (magnetic resonance imaging) machine took pictures of my heart and lungs. The bed moved, and I was pulled into a long noisy tube-like machine with a bright overhead light. I attempted to make myself comfortable by slowly counting my breaths.

Moving my eyes from the left to the right side of my body, I counted seven orbs of colored light. Shades of red, orange, yellow, green, blue, indigo, and violet hovered around me. They lengthened and grew. As I looked at each of the colors, I knew at once that they were angels sent to guide me.

A deep green aura at my feet looked to be alive. As I watched it weave and swirl, the shape of the orb changed into a living, jungle-like web of leaves and vines. The noise of the MRI machine blended into the vines and echoed back to me. I felt as though I were in a lush green jungle filled with exotic birds and beautiful flowers. I knew an angel had to be creating this living, moving green aura, but the colors and sounds attracted so much of my attention that I hardly noticed the angel stepping out from behind the foliage. She smiled at me and told me to breathe. Birds flew all around her. Long, beautiful snakes and lizards camouflaged themselves in the hanging vines. A gentle lion sat beneath her right hand. I knew this woman had to be Archangel Ariel.

"Close your eyes and let me take you away from this," she whispered. Suggesting I lose myself in the sweet song of the birds, Archangel Ariel's presence calmed my senses. In that moment, the noise and any lasting fear I had vanished. I could relax! I could breathe.

In angel society, Archangel Ariel is the Lion/Lioness of God. Representing the side of God that is strong and courageous, she is connected to everything on this earth, including you and me.

Archangel Ariel is the overseer of sprites, fairies, and nymphs. So if you enjoy spending time outdoors, investigating the natural world, listening to the birds, watching the animals, or drawing the fairies, you'll love this archangel!

An Angel Is an Angel—No Matter How Small

This may sound like Dr. Seuss talking, but take care. Watch where you are walking! Ariel's presence is strongest in the sky, trees, water, and amongst the animals of the earth. Her helper angels are tending to every flower, creature, and blade of grass. Have you ever seen a brightly colored bug buzzing around a flowerbed or flowerpot only to have it fly away when you try to get a closer look?

"It was there just a second ago!" you tell yourself. So where could it have gone? Chances are you are one of the fortunate people to have just seen a fairy.

These tiny fairies and sprites are guardian angels. Caring for everything in nature, they can be a pinpoint of light darting past your eyes or a bit of dust drifting through the air. At least one guardian angel watches over you every single day and all through the night. So the next time you see something floating through the air, don't be surprised if it's your own personal fairy godmother!

Not only is Archangel Ariel the overseer of sprites, fairies, and nymphs, she also lends an angelic hand to assist the mammals, birds, reptiles, and fish! You can call on Archangel Ariel to help you care for your pets, watch over the flowers in your garden, and encourage your fruit trees and vegetable plants to grow. If you're interested in getting involved with environmental issues such as keeping our lakes and rivers clean or saving our rainforests, Archangel Ariel is the angel you'll want to call upon.

No matter the weather, Archangel Ariel will show you the wonders and beauty of our great earth. With Ariel by your side, you will discover a newfound appreciation for all of God's creatures. If you're not sure how to talk to Archangel Ariel, it's really quite simple. Just call her name! Simply ask her to help you to better see our world from her point of view. But remember, if you ask for Archangel Ariel's help, you must be prepared to receive all of the cheerful and loving thoughts she will send your way!

Ariel's Prayer for You

Archangel Ariel is always listening. Even now, she waits for your call. Simply begin by saying:

God, with Archangel Ariel by my side, please help me to see a world filled with blue skies, happy creatures, and pure love.

Call Ariel using these words any time—and as often as you like—until you are comfortable enough to call on her using your own words. Archangel Ariel never tires of hearing from her earth angels. *That's you!*

Meeting Archangel Ariel's Nature Angels

Now that you know a little about Archangel Ariel, grab a picnic lunch, and let's go outside to look for her and her choirs. Anywhere you are in nature, Ariel is there too! You can even start in your own backyard! If you don't have a backyard, ask Mom or Dad to plan a special time to take you to the park so you can be close to the trees and small animals. Once there, get ready to go on an Archangel Ariel scavenger hunt! Are you ready?

Besides your nourishing snack of fresh or dried fruit, cheese with bread or crackers, and cool fresh water, you may like to bring a clipboard and pencil, but it's not at all important for finding Ariel and her choir of angels. In fact, the only real tools you will need for this scavenger hunt already belong to you. I'm talking about your senses! Sight, touch, smell, hearing, and of course that invisible sense called intuition.

Begin by using your ability to listen well. Do you know that you can connect with angels quickly and easily by using your ears? This simple method of *listening* for the angel's messages is called *Clear Hearing*.

Get ready, get set, get comfortable outside on the grass, in a lawn chair, or in a tree. (Just don't climb too high. You'll be closing your eyes!) Take a slow, deep breath through your nose. This is the best way of filling your stomach with fresh, clean air.

Can you see your tummy growing? Good! Now close your eyes and gently blow the air out of your stomach in a long, slow stream through your mouth. Imagine you are blowing a huge pink bubble. Listen to the sounds around you.

Inhale slowly to fill your stomach once again.

Exhale slowly to let the air out.

Inhale. Place your hand on your tummy so that you can feel it growing.

Exhale. Keep your hand on your tummy so that you can feel it getting smaller.

Can you hear the sound of nature? It's all around you!

Make a mental checklist of the sounds you hear. Below is a list of some of the things you might hear. Feel free to add your own ideas if what you hear is not listed below:

♥	*Animals scampering*	♥	*Bees buzzing*
♥	*Birds calling*	♥	*Birds singing*
♥	*Butterflies fluttering*	♥	*Cars passing*
♥	*Cats mewing*	♥	*Cicadas droning*
♥	*Crickets chirping*	♥	*Ducks quacking*

♥	*Dogs barking*	♥	*Flies swarming*
♥	*Frogs croaking*	♥	*Leaves blowing*
♥	*Mosquitoes humming*	♥	*People laughing*
♥	*Squirrels chattering*	♥	*You Breathing*
♥	*Water running*	♥	*Wind chimes*
♥	*Wings flapping*	♥	*Wind whispering*

Open your eyes. How many birds did you hear calling? How many squirrels did you hear chattering in the trees? How many dogs did you count barking?

Make a list of the sounds you heard. You can write them down or just call them out. When you are done, thank Archangel Ariel for revealing herself to you. Saying something like this helps:

*Archangel Ariel, thank you for helping me to
clearly hear all the sounds of nature.*

Remember, when you listen this way, you are using your *Clear Hearing*. It's the best way to hear Archangel Ariel's nature songs. Now take a break. Have a nibble of your food or a cool drink of your water. Lie down in the grass and watch the clouds float by. Or you might want to ask Mom and Dad to take a walk with you. Perhaps you can teach them how to use their *Clear Hearing!*

More Ways to Connect with Archangel Ariel

The next time you wish to connect with Archangel Ariel, you may choose to use only your sense of sight to see all this angel of courage has to offer. This is the skill of *Clear Seeing*. To do this, you will need to put your fingers in your ears. Make sure they are plugged so you cannot hear the sounds around you. Now close your eyes!

Some people only use their eyes to see. Others can actually "see" clearer when they use their intuition. Archangel Ariel tells us it is quite natural for two people to look at one thing and see it in completely different ways. Now that you know this, practice *Clear Seeing*.

Breathe softly and count the number of birds you sense around you. Now open your eyes and look around. Unplug your ears and listen. How did you do? Do you see more birds in your mind or with your eyes? Does it help for you to hear the birds as well as see them?

Practice *Clear Seeing* with insects. How many insects can you sense around you? How many small animals do you sense foraging for nuts and playing in the trees? You can use your *Clear Seeing* to find dogs, cats, even lions if you like! Archangel Ariel loves lions!

There are two other clear senses you might like to try. These are *Clear Feeling* and *Clear Knowing*. With *Clear Feeling*, you can actually feel the presence of a creature before you see it. Intuition is the feeling you have that tells you one of Archangel Ariel's nature angels is near. That's why even those who are blind are usually able to see quite clearly in their mind's eye.

Clear Knowing is thinking of an animal and, all of a sudden, it is standing there in front of you! If you find it easier to use your clear senses while outside, Ariel suggests you thank the fairies and sprites for that!

Fairy aura can be any color, but rose, violet, green, yellow, and white tend to be their favorites. They can sometimes look like tiny hummingbirds or miniature humans with wings, but the truth is a fairy is so small that it may just appear to you as a part of nature. A fairy could look like a small particle of light, a tiny butterfly, or a seed floating in the air. So the next time a speck floats past your eye, take a quick look! It may, in fact, be a fairy telling you to stop, look, and listen to the sounds of the natural world around you. And when you do this, always remember to do so with kindness.

Archangel Ariel commonly shows herself surrounded by an aura of pink and earth tone colors. When I saw Ariel in the MRI lab, she was hidden in a brilliant green aura instead. These were her nature angels. Legions and legions of tiny sprite-like angels hovered in her hair, around her body, and in front of her face. There were so many of them that, when they came together, these speck-sized angels created a picture of a jungle just for me! Whispering to me to immerse myself in the sounds, smells, and feelings of nature, I was able to relax and even enjoy the long, painful test.

Archangel Ariel says, "When you think of the air, think of Ariel! My nature angels and I love to connect with most of you when you are outside. But we are not fussy about how we do it. We'll spend time with you just about anywhere you are most relaxed."

Now that you know that Archangel Ariel guides us through nature, let's meet some more archangels who guide us through life!

To remember Ariel, think about the first part of her name. Ari'el is an Air Angel.

Archangel Ariel and her Nature Angels with original sketch in oval.

This angel lion/lioness belongs to the Schemhamphoras (Schem/ham/phor/as), a select group of angels who hold the name of God. Bold ruler over the sign of Leo, this blazing Archangel of Fire guides all who honor Mother Earth, including the fairies and sprites charged with caring for the animals of our world.

CHAPTER 3

Archangel Azrael

Whom God Helps

Azrael whispers to you, "I am with you always, dear child. You need not call my name to feel my loving presence by your side. When you are sad, frightened, ill, or lonely, I am with you.

It had been a long time since my parents last tucked me into bed. I was fifteen years old. *Too old,* I thought as they patted the blankets around me. They looked very worried as they said their goodnights. And why shouldn't they have been worried? This was the night before my first open heart surgery.

Once my parents were gone, I went into the bathroom and looked at myself in the mirror. "You will never look like this again," I told myself.

Placing my hand on my chest, I tried to imagine what it would be like to have a thin scar running down the front of my smooth skin. Fighting back the tears, I crawled into bed and fell into a deep, peaceful sleep.

It felt as though only a second had passed when I awoke. At first, I thought the early morning sunshine was beginning to peek through my hospital room window. The room was quiet and calm. Even though the doctors would be doing open heart surgery on me in a few hours, I felt calm and relaxed.

"That's impossible," I told myself when I heard the sound of the birds singing outside my window. Having spent most of my childhood in the hospital, I knew that the double-paned windows shut out the noises from outside. This included the sound of the birds chirping. Opening my eyes, I saw a shining yellow light fall across one half of my room. This light was so bright that I could not see into the other half of the room. The window had become completely covered with light.

I couldn't exactly hear any words, but the strange light seemed to say, "Set aside your fears, oh child of God. You are safe."

You might think I would have been scared, but I wasn't. I somehow knew it was one of God's messengers.

My parents arrived a few hours later with the same concerned look in their eyes. They held my hands and walked beside my stretcher as far as the elevators.

"Don't worry," I told them. "I'll be back before you know it!"

My mother praised me for being so calm, but I had no reason to be scared. I knew that Archangel Azrael and my guardian angels were with me. I was safe. I was ready. I knew something my parents did not. There was no doubt in my mind that I would come out of the surgery stronger and healthier.

It's hard not to be sad at the thought of someone you love dying. You feel as if you can't see them or talk to them or play with them anymore. You might even feel left behind when their spirit goes to heaven.

Imagine you are a turtle. Like a turtle, you carry your real self deep inside a protective outer shell. This shell is your body. Just like a turtle, your body is home to that hidden part of you called your spirit. At times, your spirit pokes out and shows itself to the world in much the same way that Mr. Turtle pokes his head out. Depending on the type of turtle he is, when his head pokes out, Mr. Turtle may move forward, have a look around, go back inside, or snap at the first thing it sees.

Our spirit acts in much the same way. Who we are shows up in our likes and dislikes. It comes through in our habits and the way we do things. It tells our mouths to smile and our eyes to cry. Like each turtle, our spirit is one of a kind, and at the same time a part of God's creation. So when the outer shell dies, your turtle inside—or your spirit—goes to a happy place where God and the angels will take care of you. Understanding this might help you to feel better about losing someone you love.

Understanding Archangel Azrael

To help you better understand Azrael's job, I'm going to tell you a story about what happened when my grandfather, the person I loved most in this world, died.

I was eighteen years old when I learned of his passing. On the day of his funeral, I placed my hand on his forehead. Even though his body was cold, I felt the warmth of his spirit all around me. I realized then that, like the turtle, the human body is just a shell. What is inside that shell lives forever.

After the funeral, I felt him standing beside me just about everywhere I went. In fact, it has been years since my grandpa's death, and I still sense his warm and loving presence sitting on the sofa beside me, hugging me when I am sad or lonely, and whispering words of love in my ear! I no longer feel sad that my grandpa has gone to heaven; instead, I feel blessed that his spirit is still connected to mine and always will be.

Archangel Azrael's Band of Mercy

If you are like me, and someone you love is in heaven, you may see sparkles of light zooming through the air when you think of that person. At the time of my grandpa's death I saw faint streams of yellow light. I know now this is a sign of Archangel Azrael's presence. I believe it was also my grandpa's way of saying, "I am still here." Years have passed since his death, but thanks to Azrael's intervention, I still feel Grandpa's spirit watching over me.

This soft-spoken, caring angel is one of my favorites. Having the same name as Gargamel's black cat in the Smurf cartoon, Azrael is thought to be no small pussycat! In fact, the *Quran* tells us that Azrael is so big he can reach from heaven to earth, and so wise that God asks him to keep track of every spirit on earth and in heaven.

Every time a baby is born, Azrael writes his or her name on a leaf from the Tree of Life. When a leaf falls from the tree, Archangel Azrael catches it as it falls and looks at the name. Sent from God to help spirits cross the bridge between heaven and earth, Azrael's job is to hold a person's hand while his or her turtle shell is dying and to show that spirit the path to heaven. But this magnificent angel doesn't stop there. Archangel Azrael comforts us by sending his band of kindhearted angels to watch over us.

Many spirits are called to join Azrael's band of angels. These spirits live with us on earth to help us live our lives in peace. For this reason, Azrael is honored by the angels in heaven and is called the angel of death on earth. But the true meaning of Azrael's name is "whom God helps." What a great way to describe the angel who comforts the dying and sends messages of hope to the people they love. Ministers, teachers, and world leaders often call on Azrael and his Band of Mercy to stand beside them when they are scared. You can too!

Feel Azrael's Light

When you are waking up in your bedroom or comfy in a favorite quiet place, you are most likely to feel Archangel Azrael's light. You might even feel a lot of other angels surrounding your bed, sending you love, peace, and happiness! Whether it's early in the morning or late at night, Azrael is always there for you. You can even talk to him in your sleep!

To call on Archangel Azrael, simply say,

> *Dear Archangel Azrael, please hold (person/pet who has passed or is dying) safe in your hands. Please lead this spirit to heaven to be with you and the angels. Please stay by my side to help my spirit be happy again.*

Archangel Azrael's Science Experiment

To take Archangel Azrael's message of helping one step further, this caring archangel challenges you to help others. Treat each day of the week like a science experiment. Before you begin, draw a pictograph in a journal or notebook. Or, if you prefer, go big! Draw one on a large piece of paper that you can sticky tack to your wall. Write the days of the week. down the side of your page and "Number of Smiles" at the top. When you are finished, it should look something like this:

☺ **Number of Smiles** ☺

Sunday
Monday
Tuesday
Wednesday
Thursday
Friday
Saturday

Azrael's Prayer for You

Before you leave your house, Archangel Azrael asks that you stop for a moment to say a prayer for kindness. This is Azrael's prayer for you:

> *Please, God, help me to see you in my eyes. Help me to see myself in the eyes of others. Help me to show my caring self to others each and every day! Please, God, help me to see kindness in this world, even if at first it's just my own.*

Each time you look at a person or animal, see your own image reflecting back at you through their eyes.
When you see love, smile and be caring.
When you see joy, smile and be caring.
When you see excitement, smile and be caring.

How many times were your caring words or actions met with kindness? Remembering that, it's easy to find kindness in a happy person, so ...
When you see sadness, show you care. Smile.
When you see frustration, show you care. Smile.
When you see anger, show you care. Smile.
When you see yourself, show you care. Smile.

How many times did your caring words or actions help turn a frown upside down? If it was one person the first day, challenge yourself the next day to turn two frowns upside down! Draw a face for every person who smiled back or was in a happier mood.

Record the results of your experiment right up until the time you go to bed. This way, you will be able to include family members in your study! At the end of the week, count how many times your caring actions created a smile or helped someone feel better. Ask yourself how many times your actions made you feel happy too.

Archangel Azrael says, "Before you drift off to sleep tonight, invite my Band of Mercy and me to come play with you in your dreams. We will surround you with our loving yellow energy and watch over your leaf throughout the night."

Close your eyes and see your leaf hanging sure and strong on the Tree of Life. Sleep well knowing that your leaf will only fall when your spirit is ready to go to heaven. On that day, Archangel Azrael will gently take your hand and guide you across the spiritual bridge.

To remember Archangel Azrael's name, think about the word "real." It is the end of this special angel's name, and reminds you that Azrael knows your "real self."

Archangel Azrael with original sketch in oval.

This angel of the third heaven, Ruler of Pluto, is rapt with reincarnation and multiple lives. Known as the caring angel, Archangel Azrael guides your soul to the gates of heaven when your body dies. When you are once again ready to take human form, Azrael celebrates the rebirth of your soul by giving you a new body.

CHAPTER 4

Archangel Chamuel

He Who Sees God

> *Archangel Chamuel whispers to you,*
> *"Search for us in everything you do. We angels are the*
> *love in your heart and the calm in your mind."*

THIS ADORED ARCHANGEL IS said to be one of the first angels God ever created! With all of his titles, Archangel Chamuel is one of the angels who sit closest to God in heaven. His main job is Keeper of the Earth. So even if it sounds like Archangel Chamuel is very far away, this all-knowing angel is always with you. Just by asking, Archangel Chamuel will take your fears away when you are scared and help you to find caring and peaceful solutions to any dispute.

Keeper of the Earth

As Keeper of the Earth, Archangel Chamuel helps you understand your world. He is protector of everything, including you! Archangel Chamuel is sometimes called "He who seeks God" because he looks for God in all people. And sometimes Archangel Chamuel is called "He who sees God" because he is always able to find God inside of you.

Archangel Chamuel says, "Nothing is ever really lost. All you seek, you will find. Just believe, and I will reveal joy in everything you do and everyone you meet!"

Do you think you may have lost something? Whether it is an overdue library book or your best friend, with Archangel Chamuel on your side, it is never really lost.

Archangel Chamuel helped me the other day while I was writing a letter. I was looking for a story from the New Testament to use in that letter, but I had no idea where to find it. Closing my eyes, I took a deep breath and asked Archangel Chamuel to please help me find the place where Jesus calls the children to him.

I smiled. Straightaway, I felt a gentle warmth fall over me. Knowing that Archangel Chamuel had rushed to my side, I opened my eyes and flipped the page over once. My eyes looked at the page. Following Archangel Chamuel's guidance, I flipped the page over one more time. Immediately, I found the story I had asked for—right there in front of my eyes!

"Thank you, Archangel Chamuel," I whispered quickly. After that, I finished writing my letter. Remembering to thank the angels tells them you are joyful for every kindness they bring.

Your Archangel Friend

Archangel Chamuel is a caring, patient angel who brings calm whenever he is near. He is a wonderful friend who can be called upon whenever you feel lonely or sad. This quiet, peaceful angel reminds us even when our lives are filled with confusion we are children of love, Children of God. So the next time you find yourself in an argument with another person, think of Archangel Chamuel. His gentle, loving presence is always available to remind you of God's universal laws. Happiness comes from inside of you. And when you look for love, you will always find it.

Inviting Chamuel into Your Life

Outside, in a bed of rosy red flowers is where many people like to call on Archangel Chamuel. I don't have a bed of red roses, so I have found the simplest way to meet with Archangel Chamuel is by simply saying, "Archangel Chamuel, I need you!" Instantly, the gentle gaze of his soft blue eyes and the warm glow of his blue-green aura engulf me.

Would you like Archangel Chamuel to come into your life? Can you feel him anywhere around you?

Make a list of the people you love and those who love you. Don't forget to include those who live far away or those you may not see anymore. Record the names of animals, favorite trees, or any other living thing you are fond of. Don't worry if you're not sure how to spell their names correctly. Archangel Chamuel knows who they are. He can read your thoughts.

After you write a name on your paper, close your eyes and picture that person standing in front of you. Remember to include animals on your list as well.

Say the person's name and tell him you love him. It really doesn't matter if you do this out loud or in your mind. Imagine you are getting a big warm hug from this person. Now watch as the person or animal moves around to the back of your chair and is standing behind you. Open your eyes and imagine the same thing happening with the next person or animal on your list. Tell the next name on your list how much you love him or her. Feel the warm, loving feeling you get when you are being hugged. As he or she moves behind your chair, go to the next name on your list. Do this again and again until you have had a visit from everyone you can think of to include on your sheet of paper.

Feel the heat of every spirit standing behind you even after you have crossed his or her name off your list. Relax as you listen to the sound of their breathing behind you. Breathe in the special scent of each person or animal. Feel the love inside your heart.

Once you have reached the end of your list, look over your shoulder to see everyone standing behind you. Use your imagination. Can you see them smiling at you? They are joined in a circle of love just for you! Feel their warmth. They are sending their love to you right now.

Pretend you are holding a camera and snap a mental picture of the group in your mind. Quickly reach for a blank piece of paper or turn your list over and draw the picture you took in your head onto the blank side. It doesn't have to be perfect. It doesn't even have to look the way you want it to look! It's the idea that counts. Hang your drawing in your room or some other place where you can see it whenever you need a reminder of how much love is in this world for you.

Chamuel's Advice to You

Archangel Chamuel says, "When you see the love in your life, we angels are there too. Each time you meet a new angel, please add us to your group of loved ones standing behind you."

If you would rather not make the angels look like angels in your picture, remember Archangel Ariel and draw them as butterflies, dragonflies, or birds fluttering around those who you have already drawn. You can portray angels any way you like. Archangel Chamuel and his Choirs of Angels can be found any place you can think of. They are always with you to care for you and every person on this earth who gives and receives love.

Prince Charming was a kindhearted prince. Like Prince Charming, Archangel Chamuel is compassionate, caring, charitable, and considerate.

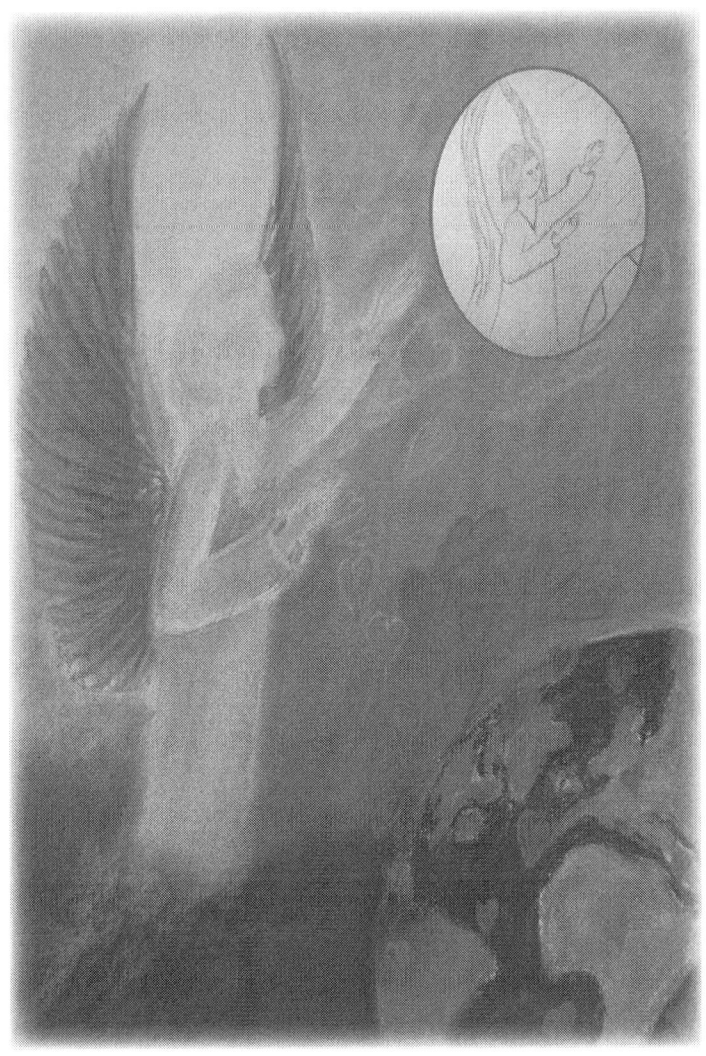

Archangel Chamuel with original sketch in oval.

As Head of the Dominions, Angel of the Presence, Prince of Seraphim, and Lead Prince of the Powers, this mighty archangel is understood to be one of God's greatest angels. Chamuel is believed to be the angel who visited Jesus in the Garden of Gethsemane just before his crucifixion. He is the Ruler of Tuesday and the planet Mars. For all of these reasons, he is believed to be one of God's favorite angels.

CHAPTER 5

Archangel Gabriel

God is My Strength

> *Archangel Gabriel whispers to you, "Come to me, all God's Children; take my hand. I am your strength. I will shelter you in my light when you are sad and lonely. I will guide your path so you understand your true power. Your power is your talents. Your talents make you who you are. By your talents, you will lead others. Use them. Enjoy them. Live by them."*

As the Angel of Birth, Archangel Gabriel guides every baby ever born into this world. By touching you on the upper lip just before you are born, she leaves a dimple on your chin. Each time you look in the mirror, glance at this small cleft. It is her reminder to you that as God's child you are rightly and entirely loved.

"God is my strength" is the meaning of Archangel Gabriel's name.

Close your eyes and think about the strongest, gentlest person or animal you can imagine. Look closely. Somewhere in your mind's eye, or that picture inside your head, you will see beautiful, powerful, loving Archangel Gabriel!

I have met this archangel many times in my life. As far back as I can remember I have felt her presence in my room—even before I knew she was an archangel. As I grew up, I felt Archangel Gabriel's strength beside me whenever I was worried about a friendship or nervous about my schoolwork. Her loving presence helped me calm down and focus on what was really important.

When I was a teacher, she helped me to speak clearly whenever I taught a lesson. With Archangel Gabriel's guidance, I was able to utterly believe in the talents of each one of my students. When I was adopting my babies, Archangel Gabriel helped me say what I needed to say to the doctors and social workers. This multi-talented archangel even led me to my career in writing.

Every so often, authors get what's called writer's block. That's when you can't think of anything to write, or you have so many ideas that you have trouble focusing on writing about just one. That's what happened to me the day I wrote this chapter! After a very busy morning, I sat down at my desk to write about an archangel, but I had so many angel ideas in my head that I couldn't settle my mind to write about just one. I simply couldn't think of how to begin or what to say!

"Please angels," I begged, "please help me find the right words. Help me to explain each angel in simple words."

I had been planning to write about another angel, but each time I started writing, something stopped me. Even though I was not working on Archangel Gabriel at the time, I kept thinking something was missing. Each time I tried to get to work, I'd get sidetracked! If that's ever happened to you, then you'll understand how frustrating it can be!

Every time I tried to get back to writing about this other angel, a little voice in my head whispered, "Why don't you write about me?" After all these years of hearing angels talk to me, you'd think I would listen to what they have to say! But on that day, I was too focused on getting my work done to take the time to listen. In time, the voice grew so strong that I couldn't ignore it anymore.

"Who are you?" I finally asked.

As soon as the question had left my lips, a deep red velvet color drifted through my mind. This is the color I have seen for the past three years each time Gabriel is around. When I was a little girl, Archangel Gabriel was encircled with many shades of blue when she came to visit. When I became a teenager, she was surrounded by an aura of misty green. And now she comes to me in deep shades of red!

At first I thought this was strange, so I asked the angels why their auras kept changing. They told me that, as you grow and change your understanding of the angels, the way you see them often changes as well. Angel colors can be a sign of how we are thinking and what we are thinking.

The angels also reminded me that they love variety! They like to change their colors in much the same way you like to change your clothes. No matter how you see your angels, don't get hung up on the color of the aura. Archangel Gabriel has shown me that everything changes in time!

Getting back to my angel-writing problem, as soon as I saw the deep red, I knew it had to be Gabriel talking.

"Okay, Archangel Gabriel," I said, sitting in my room with my laptop open. "What would you like me to say?" And so my chapter on this persistent angel began!

When my head was too heavy to hold up and my brain felt too tired to think, I gave in and allowed Archangel Gabriel to take over. As God's favorite messenger of good news, it's no wonder that Archangel Gabriel is also the writer's helper! Now, every time I sit down to write, I feel her sitting directly beside me. In fact, I can hear her whispering in my ear as I type my words. My only job is to listen!

The History of Archangel Gabriel

Before you begin your conversation with Archangel Gabriel, I'll tell you a little more about this incredible angel.

In Luke 1:11–33 of the King James Bible, Saint Luke tells us about Archangel Gabriel. Called the Gospel according to Luke, this section made Gabriel famous! In it, he names Gabriel as the angel who told the Virgin Mary she would be giving birth to the baby Jesus.

Further on, Luke 1:57–63, Archangel Gabriel speaks to Mary's uncle, an older man called Zacharias. She appeared to him while he was speaking to God in a Jewish place of worship called a temple. Gabriel told Zacharias that he and his wife would have a baby and that they'd name the baby John. Zacharias did not believe what Archangel Gabriel said was possible. He told the angel that his wife was too old to have a baby and he was too old to raise a child.

True to Archangel Gabriel's word, Zacharias's wife, Elizabeth, gave birth to a strong and healthy baby boy nine months later! In front of all his family and friends, Zacharias announced his name would be John.

Now John may not seem like a strange name to you, but it was for Zacharias. Back in his time, a son was always named after his father or another close male relative. In his story, Saint Luke tells us that until Baby John was born, nobody with that name had ever been a member of either Zacharias's or Elizabeth's family.

Six months later, Elizabeth's cousin Mary, the same Virgin Mary I spoke of before, gave birth to Baby Jesus in a town called Bethlehem. What is really interesting is that shepherds in the fields and wise men traveling by camel to Bethlehem said that they had seen choirs of angels in the sky on the same night Jesus was born.

Can you guess the name of the angel that came down from the heavens to tell them about his birth? That's right. It was Gabriel! To this day, Archangel Gabriel is the most famous of all of God's messengers.

In the angelic realm, Gabriel is the kind and gentle leader of spiritual beings called the Cherubim. She holds one of the highest chairs in heaven where her Cherubim sit around God. This choir of angels sees everything and knows everything. They even know all about you! With Archangel Gabriel as their leader, the Cherubim spread God's love to all people.

Calling on Gabriel and her Cherubim

Gabriel and her Cherubim are happy to help you with anything from writing a story for your teacher to writing a book for the whole world to read! Call on her whenever you need to gather and write down your ideas. She will be very happy to lend a hand. You can also call on Archangel Gabriel if you have speech problems or if you need to talk to someone but don't know how to begin. Even though Gabriel knows all, you must ask for her help before she can help you to follow your great path on this earth. The very best way I have found to call on Archangel Gabriel is through writing.

Grab a ruled piece of paper, a diary, or a notebook and write the very first thought that pops into your head. You can doodle or simply draw circles—as long as you say the following out loud or silently:

> *Archangel Gabriel, I call on you to help me with (name whatever it is you need help with here. It could be completing a school project, it could be speaking openly to your parents, or it could be introducing yourself to an interesting new friend). Please shower me with your strength of spirit, your clear and simple words, and your heavenly guidance.*
>
> *Please surround me with your Cherubim so they may watch over me and see what I cannot. Please guide me to communicate clearly in my thoughts, actions, and words. Thank you, thank you gentle, yet mighty angel.*
>
> *Once you have grown accustom to speaking to Archangel Gabriel on a regular basis, you may begin using your own words to call on this mighty communicator of God.*
>
> *Play with the word "baby." Babe rhymes with Gabe. Now you will remember Archangel Gabriel's name and at least one mission of this creatively nurturing archangel.*

Archangel Gabriel with original sketch in oval.

Sitting at the left hand of God, this Angel of Justice oversees the first and sixth heaven. Believed to be a leading member of the Sarim, the earliest group of angels to repeatedly sing praises to God, Archangel Gabriel is also Ruler of Cherubim and Princess of the Virtues. She is the Patron of light, revelation, truth, and surprisingly, war. Lilies symbolize the presence of this peaceful archangel, God's most popular messenger.

CHAPTER 6

Archangel Haniel

The Grace of God

> *Archangel Haniel whispers to you, "When you are tired, we will help you sleep. When you are sad, we will hold your hand. Close your eyes and be transported to a world filled with joy. When you are angry, please come. We breathe into you the peace of the universe and our Lord God."*

I met Archangel Haniel in my mind's eye while walking through a beautiful, lavender-filled garden. It was late at night, but Haniel had something to show me. She took my hand and led me down a stone path, further into the garden. In the center where the trees broke into an open star-filled sky, Archangel Haniel instructed me to look up into the light of the full moon.

"I love the moonlight!" Haniel proclaimed with genuine pleasure.

"Why do you love the moon?" I asked.

She took a deep breath and said, "Because the moon is forgiving."

I wondered how a moon could be forgiving. It's just a giant piece of rock in the sky. But as I started to ask Archangel Haniel what made the moon so forgiving, she led my mind to discover the answer for myself.

Its bright, intense light shone down on us, casting a cerulean glow all around. The sleeping world seemed so calm and at peace. Immediately, I knew.

Haniel looked at me and smiled. "Yes!" she said in a soft, breathless voice. "The moon brings peace!"

Standing in the garden, holding Haniel's hand, I was surrounded by darkness. I saw and felt the light of the universe. Drowsy from her touch, I drank in the fragrant scents and soft subtle lilac and violet tones throughout the garden. I closed my eyes.

Haniel said, "Breathe deeply, my child. For with every breath, you find peace."

Finding Archangel Haniel

Many angel researchers report that the best way to find Haniel is by going outside on a moon-filled night. If you have ever been to a cottage or a beach after dark, you may already understand Haniel's message of peace. On a clear night, when the moon is shining off of the water, the whole world seems alight with the harmony of that calm.

The next time you are outside camping or near water, look up at the moon and feel this gentle archangel's presence all around you. A silvery haze of deep purple on the water, over the moon, or far off in the distance is an indication that Haniel is near.

You don't need to see her color to feel her presence. That sleepy feeling you get from taking slow, steady breaths, from listening to the crickets sing, or the water move is another indication that Haniel is with you.

Haniel's Grace

Haniel says, "Gaze into the moonlight and breathe deeply three times. Look at the darkness all around you, then back to the moon high in the sky, and you will see that the night is not dark or gloomy. Rejoice! The night is filled with silvery linings and soft purple moors! The night is filled with the light of the moon. Gaze into that light, and we will be there."

Can you feel her peace? Next time you are outside, take her hand and let God's Grace wash over you.

For those of you who would rather not go outside alone, that's okay! Haniel loves it when people come together. She loves to see families enjoying each other's company. Most of all, she loves to see you relax and smile.

Remember that Archangel Haniel can easily come to you in your sleep. If you can't get outdoors, close your eyes and think about standing outside. You could be in your backyard, on a beach, or anywhere in the world! Pick your favorite place and see yourself standing there. Breathe deeply and ask Archangel Haniel to join you.

You may whisper, *Archangel Haniel, please visit me in my sleep or while I am daydreaming. Smile with me so that I too may look at the light of the moon and the peace of God that you bring to the night. Thank you for being with me, Haniel. Thank you for grace. Thank you for showing me the light of any dark night.*

Archangel Haniel is a beautiful, quiet angel. Her soft, pleasing voice and slow, peaceful manner can help you relax and feel sleepy. She breathes soothing thoughts into your ideas and transfers feelings of loving calm to those who call on her. This "Grace of God" is best known for coming to us in our dreams. Call on her nightly and ask her to bring peace to all that you do.

> *Archangel Haniel is the archangel associated with the moon.*
> *This young, playful angel extends her hand to you each night*
> *so you may dance with her in the moonlight. See her hand*
> *reach for yours, and you will remember Haniel's name.*

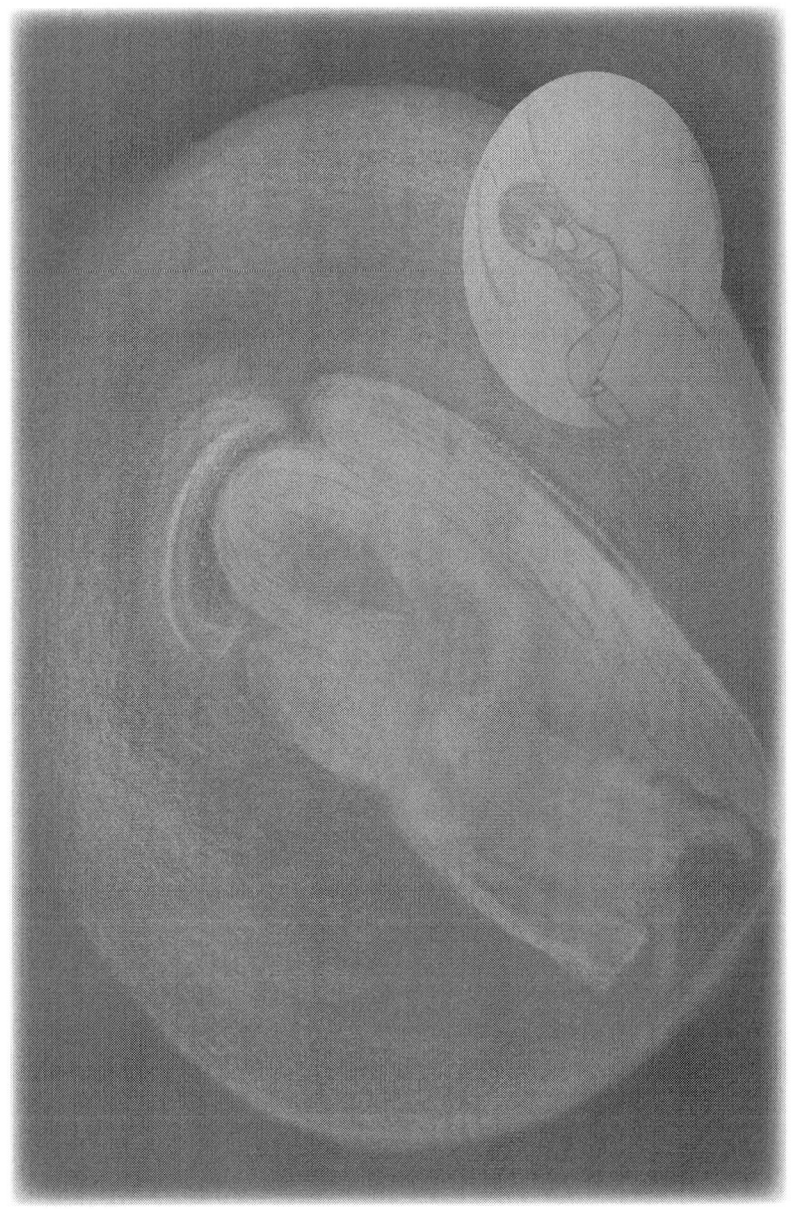

Archangel Haniel with original sketch in oval.

Believed to be one of the ten main archangels, this angel is the Ruler of Principalities and a member of the Virtues. She is a planetary angel who is also thought to have transported Enoch to heaven.

CHAPTER 7

Archangel Jeremiel

The Mercy of God

Archangel Jeremiel whispers to you, "As we shed mercy on you, dear child, you must shed mercy on yourself."

WHEN I WAS A young girl, the very idea of being visited by a spirit or ghost was too awful to even imagine. That was until the night I had an unexpected visit from a very good friend.

It was nearly two o'clock in the morning, and the room was pitch-dark when I jolted awake from a sound sleep. Rolling onto my back, I looked up to see my close friend, Shawn, standing at the foot of my bed. In my sleepy state, I was happy to see him, even if he was standing in my room in the middle of the night! But as my head cleared and I became fully alert, I thought about the accident that had taken Shawn from his family and friends just a few nights before. At once, I realized that what I was seeing was Shawn's spirit!

With a shriek, I pulled my covers up around my face. Feeling my dread, he quickly faded away. Shawn had simply come to say good-bye. His quick disappearance clearly told me that he had no intentions of scaring me. It was me who frightened him with my screams!

After that night, I felt there had to be more to spirits roaming the earth than the horror-movie idea of ghosts looking for a person to frighten. Night after night, I hoped Shawn would revisit. From time to time, I'd feel his presence and sense his message of love, but he never visually showed himself to me again. Thanks to Shawn, I now have a better understanding of God's two worlds, the human one and the world of spirit.

As discussed in the section on Archangel Azrael's Band of Mercy (see Chapter 3), bands of angels rush to your side moments, hours, and even weeks before your death. Their job is to prepare you and help you prepare those you love for your passing.

In Shawn's case, throughout his life, he was never one to say what he felt in his heart. But only a few hours before his death, Shawn did something very odd. He was running out the door after having an argument with his mother. As his hand reached for the door handle, he turned back, kissed her cheek, and said, "I love you, Mom." These were his last words to her!

Stepping in before Shawn's accident, Archangel Jeremiel would have encouraged my friend to kiss his mom and tell her what was in his heart. When Shawn finally left, this gentle archangel would have lead thousands of guardian angels out the door with him. Archangel Jeremiel and his choir helped Shawn say his earthly good-byes. But much more than that, Archangel Jeremiel stayed with Shawn until Azrael arrived to lead his soul across the spiritual bridge and into heaven.

Are We Ever Ready to Leave Our World?

It is Archangel Jeremiel's job to help humans take a good look at their lives and see the love they have brought to those around them. That night in my dark bedroom, he helped Shawn do that.

Each day for weeks after his death, I asked myself if Shawn was ready to go. In the end, I decided that he must have been. And then I wondered if I'd be ready when it was my turn.

I don't remember my answer back then, but I do now. Each day I do my best to be selfless and share the talents God gave me. Knowing that I will leave this world having done some good, death and dying no longer scare me. I can say this with certainty after having prepared for a life-threatening surgery in March of 2012. Archangels Jeremiel and Azrael walked with me every step of the way.

During the time leading up to my surgery, Archangel Jeremiel told me, "The simple act of love and forgiveness for others as well as yourself is all you need to do to leave this world a better place."

Just as it is Archangel Azrael's job to catch your soul as it leaves this earth, it is Archangel Jeremiel's job to tend to you during times of great change. Known as "Mercy of God," Archangel Jeremiel will make it easy for you to remember everything you have done on this earth by keeping a record of your life from the moment you were born until the moment your spirit leaves this world.

Jeremiel's Prayer for You

One day while I was writing, Archangel Jeremiel delivered this prayer to me so quickly that I hardly remember him whispering it in my ear or guiding my hands to write it down! What I do recall is Archangel Jeremiel telling me of his wish to share it with you. Each night, just before you drift off to sleep, repeat these words softly to yourself:

> *Oh bountiful, merciful God, thank you for your eternal love.*
> *Thank you for seeing all of my mistakes and loving me anyway.*
> *Thank you for helping me to see your wondrous light just as you*
> *forever see it in me.*

You are an earth angel sent to this world to spread the spirit of love! Find your talent and use it to spread your own blessings to the world. You don't need to invite Archangel Jeremiel and his prophetic angels into your life for them to appear, but it's the polite thing to do!

Meeting Archangel Jeremiel

One of the best ways to show Archangel Jeremiel that you would like his guidance is by keeping a review of everything you do. At the beginning of each month, go over all the things you have accomplished in the previous month. Now make a list of the things you would like to accomplish in the month ahead. Some of your ideas may take little effort, and some may be quite challenging!

Record your thoughts in a journal or on a personal calendar. Draw a picture of how you will look when you have completed your biggest challenge. This is your victory.

When you wake up each day, look at the victory you have drawn and go over your list of challenges. At the end of each month, see how you did—and begin the process again for the next month. Be clear on the tasks you think you can accomplish right now and the ones that will take a little more time; don't worry if you don't finish everything on the list.

Some goals require more time and effort than others do. The tasks that are left on your list at the end of the month can be easily moved to your next list and completed in the months to come. You can even ask a brother, sister, or close friend to join you in completing some of these tasks. Why not invite your entire family to create an accomplishment calendar together!

Perhaps the happy faces and light moods of those who gain from your actions will be reward enough, but Archangel Jeremiel says, "Don't forget to reward yourself at the end of each month."

With all the amazing talents you have developed, your spirit will be free to enjoy life. Those closest to you will see your true talents shine; with Archangel Jeremiel on your side, you will always have a choir of angels ready to help the world open its eyes to your outstanding self!

Archangel Jeremiel wishes to remind you of how wonderful you are. Listen to the voice inside your head that tells you to be kind.

This is the voice of God. Hear the word "me" in Archangel Jeremiel's name, and you will remember this angel's message that God is in you!

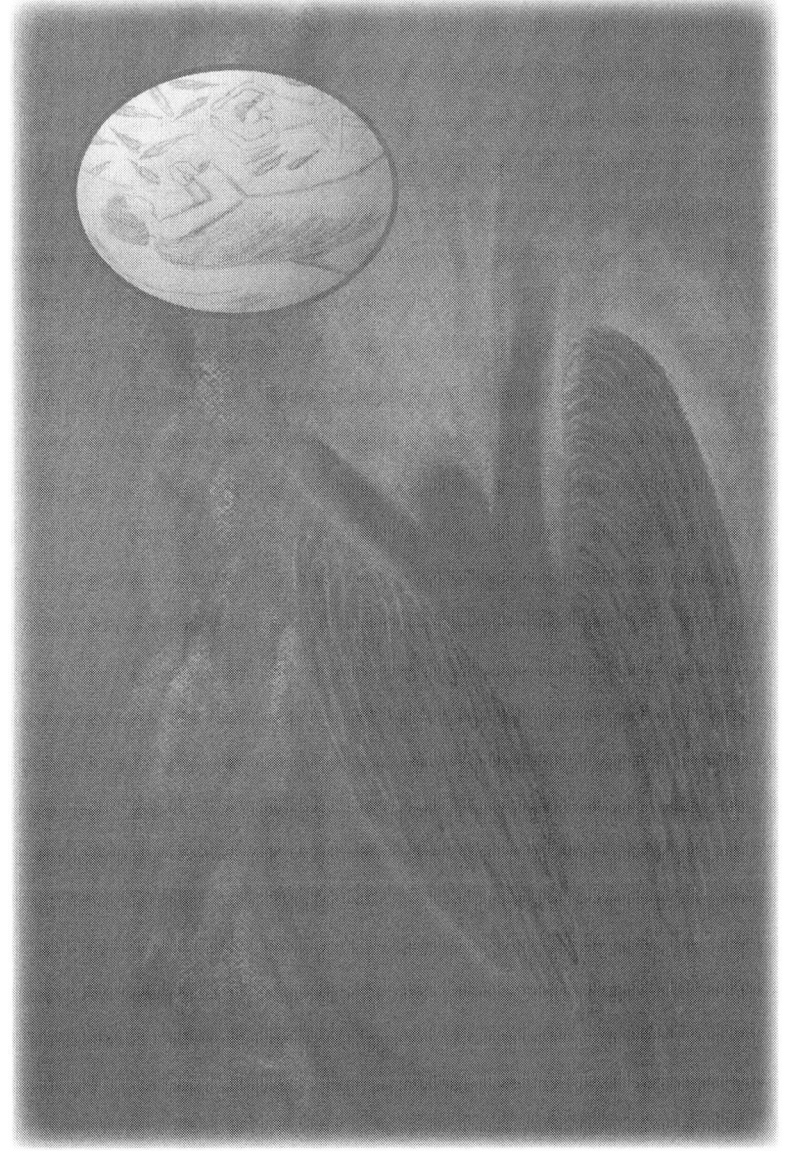

Archangel Jeremiel with original sketch in oval.

This mysterious archangel is called Ramiel in many cultures. He is known best for his work with a historical writer named Baruch. Thought to be a seer of the future soon after Jesus walked the earth, Baruch's messages are said to have come from visions of Archangel Jeremiel. Connected to Archangels Michael, Gabriel, and Uriel, this angel is considered one of the seven core archangels in heaven.

CHAPTER 8

Archangel Jophiel

The Beauty of God

> *Archangel Jophiel whispers to you, "What are we if not beautiful? Beauty is all around us. Beauty is inside of us. Beauty is God within us."*

I AM SORRY TO SAY that I didn't know about Jophiel until I began learning about the archangels. Meaning "God's beauty," Jophiel is a mighty angel who shows herself to us in the lovely things we see every day.

During my first meeting with Jophiel, I discovered very quickly that she is an angel of very few words. It's not that she cannot speak; instead, Jophiel challenges us to hear the beauty of this world rather than clutter it with unnecessary conversation.

Jophiel asks that we use our words to bring forth the beauty that is already present. Words of kindness, words of love, and words of praise are Jophiel's sounding tools. Beauty can be found in laughter, in song, and in the whispering of the wind.

The Joy of Jophiel

As you become more aware of Jophiel's influential role in your world, you will begin to see and create joy wherever you go. Archangel Jophiel tells us to find God's beauty in every flower, tree, animal, and person we meet. By doing this, you will wipe out prejudice and bullying—and never allow snootiness to exist in your world again!

Seeing beauty in your life is the key to being aware of God's message of love. When you see beauty in all living things, you will:

- Show kindness to everyone you meet,
- Take care not to hurt other people's feelings,

- See the importance of all God's creatures,
- Care for Mother Earth, including her lakes, forests, and wildlife,
- Stand up for others without causing injury,
- See yourself, and others, as you truly are, part of God's Sonship.

Calling Archangel Jophiel

Jophiel is the artists' angel. The best way to find Archangel Jophiel is to pick up a sketchpad and some colored pencils. She loves it when you draw, paint, or create in any way you enjoy. So depending on your choice of medium, you may use crayons, paints, or any other drawing tool. Call on Jophiel to help you see the beauty of your own artwork. Allow her to take your hand and guide each stroke. Your creation is her pleasure.

Be sure you have an area in the house where you can make a mess without creating a lot of chaos! If you can, sit quietly in your bedroom or a place outside where you will not be disturbed. Lay your sketchpad in your lap or on a flat surface. Lay seven colored pencils in a row close to your printing hand. As you place each pencil beside you, look at its color. First select a red pencil, next orange, next yellow, next green, next sky blue, then navy blue, and finally, find a lilac or soft purple colored pencil.

When all of your tools are ready, pick up the red pencil and close your eyes. Counting backward from seven, use all of your other senses. Begin counting:

7 - Imagine the color red. Can you hear red? Can you smell red? Can you taste red?

6 - Imagine the color orange. Can you hear orange? Can you smell orange? Can you taste orange?

5 - Imagine the color yellow. Can you hear yellow? Can you smell yellow? Can you taste yellow?

4 - Imagine the color green. Can you hear green? Can you smell green? Can you taste green?

3 - Imagine the color sky blue. Can you hear sky blue? Can you smell sky blue? Can you taste sky blue?

2 - Imagine the color navy blue. Can you hear navy blue? Can you smell navy blue? Can you taste navy blue?

1 - Imagine the color of lilac. Can you hear lilac? Can you smell lilac? Can you taste lilac?

With each new color, pick up the corresponding pencil and sketch whatever is in your thoughts. Call upon Archangel Jophiel to help you see the messages in the colors of your drawings. You may begin by saying:

Archangel Jophiel, please surround me with your rose-colored light. Help me to hear the sounds that make my heart sing, allowing all others to fall away. Help me to see the beauty deep inside of me. Help me to know my true spirit.

Allow your stunning rainbow of color to explode on your paper. When you create in Archangel Jophiel's presence, you can let go of pleasing others with your work and discover the beauty that is inside of you. Freely create!

Some people say you will know Archangel Jophiel is near when you smell the sweet smell of fragrant roses or see a bright rosy hue. I have found the easiest way of knowing she is present is by becoming aware of the beauty in your life. From the second you reach out to Archangel Jophiel, you will be amazed at the beautiful things that jump out in front of you every single day, especially your own beautiful face!

In closing, Archangel Jophiel requests that you smile at yourself in the mirror at least once a day. When you comb your hair in the morning or brush your teeth at night, take a close look. Get closer … closer … now smile! Look deeply into your own divine eyes and follow the guidance of this beautiful angel. This is how you will begin to discover your own true beauty.

When you see your beauty, you find your joy. Remember your joy, and you will remember Archangel Jophiel's name.

Archangel Jophiel with original sketch in oval.

This incredible archangel is one of the seven main archangels who is said to be guardian of the Tree Of Life. As member of the Sarim and Ruler of Thrones and Princess of the Cherubim, she uses her beautiful voice to give thanks to God. Here on earth, this charming angel shares her talent as patron of artists.

CHAPTER 9

Archangel Metatron

The Message of God

Archangel Metatron whispers to you, "Call on us angels, children of God. Shout your message of love for all to hear. Show the world your blessed talents, and find your peace."

IMAGINE A REALLY SMART, really loving grandfather who knows everything there is to know about you and every other person on this earth. In your mind's eye, can you picture hanging out with him? Can you imagine what he could teach you about yourself? If you can, then you have probably already met Archangel Metatron.

From Boy to Man to Angel

Many, many years ago, before computers, or televisions, or even books, an ordinary boy lived on this earth. Before Bahaullah, Krishna, Jesus, Buddha, or even Moses was born, there was Enoch. As a boy, Enoch loved God very much, and he wanted to learn all there was to know about his universe. But Enoch's world was filled with war.

Enoch was just about your age when Mother Earth rumbled in sorrow. His people had turned mean. Enoch watched in horror as his community began to do terrible things to one another. Before long, he feared for his life and decided the only thing he could do was hide away from everyone.

To keep his mind busy and his heart from becoming lonely, Enoch spent his time learning the secrets of God's love. He recorded everything he learned and, when he grew into a man, he became a scribe. That is what modern people call a writer.

Seeing his loyalty to God, another archangel named Raziel rewarded Enoch with a very special book. Called the Book of Raziel (see Chapter 13), this secret journal is said to be filled with God's words and symbols.

When God learned of Raziel's gift to Enoch, he asked his archangels to summon Enoch to heaven. Once in heaven, the archangels showed Enoch all the angelic realms. When God was certain Enoch had seen everything he needed to see, the archangels returned him to his home so he could write down everything he had seen and heard. These writings are now called, *The Books of Enoch*, one of the first sets of books ever written.

When Enoch died, the spirits of he and his brother Elijah rose to the heavens. Knowing of their kindheartedness toward others, God asked them to stay with the angels in heaven and become spokes-angels or archangels for you and me and all of humanity on earth. Enoch and Elijah agreed and, to this day, are believed to be the only two humans ever to have their spirits become archangels.

Enoch became the archangel called Metatron, and his brother Elijah became an archangel called Sandalphon (see Chapter 14). Remembering always that they were once children of this earth, they are committed to helping you find joy in your world and your friend to find joy in his. As brother angels, Metatron and Sandalphon work as one to help you understand that you are surrounded by angels. God is one with you.

During Enoch's transformation from human to archangel, he grew as big as our earth. His entire body became a burning flame! As an angel, Enoch, now Metatron, understands you as no other angel does. Filled with energy and divine love for all who live on this earth, Metatron's greatest love is for you, your friends, and all the children of the world.

People who study holy books say that the name Metatron means "walks with God." Others say it means "he who sits in the throne next to the Divine." And another group of really smart people call Metatron the "Angel of the Presence." Given his kindhearted nature, I don't really think Metatron cares much what you call him—as long as you call on him when you need him. Whatever name you choose, one thing is for certain: Metatron is one of the great archangels.

Talking to Archangel Metatron

If you have difficulty in school or find it hard to listen to adult rules, use words like these to ask Metatron and his guardian angels for help:

> *Dear Archangel Metatron, thank you for always being with me. Thank you helping me to see just how important my differences are, and for helping me to find joy in my habits. Please, Archangel Metatron, guide me always to be able to speak up for myself and others. Please help my words to be kind and always bring about the highest good for all. Thank you.*

In his role as Chief of Guardian Angels of the Nations, Metatron extends his invitation to you.

> "Come, march to a different drum. See the world with your eyes instead of the way others wish you to see it. Love all that is of this world, and give freely of yourself. Do not fuss if others find fault in your acts and deeds. You are a gift from the heavens. God knows what's in your heart."

Enoch did a great job of recording everything he learned about God while he was human. Now, in his angel form, God has granted him the ability to see everything that is happening in all of the heavens and on earth! In addition to instructing his guardian angels to watch over us, Archangel Metatron continues to be a scribe in heaven. That means he is always watching over you and recording everything you do!

Imagine your teacher asking you to go home and watch everything that is going on in your house and then write a report to present to the principal the next day!

"Don't leave anything out," your teacher tells you. "Everything—every little detail—is important."

Could you do it?

Archangel Metatron's Challenge to You

Archangel Metatron invites you to give it a try. Grab a camera, video recorder, or pad of paper and pencil and keep a record of everything that is happening around you. Try it for a weekend, try it at school, or try it when you are visiting a friend. How much of what you are experiencing can you write down?

Once you have spent a few days keeping track of everything in *your* world, you'll have a small idea of the job Metatron has been assigned to do by God. Imagine keeping a record of everything going on in the heavens and on this earth every day, for all of eternity! Wow!

It's a pretty big job, but as big as it is, Archangel Metatron says, "I have all the time in the world for you, my wise and talented child of God."

Consider what it would be like to "meet" Archangel Met-atron. Think Meta-drum, and start marching to your own beat!

Archangel Metatron with original sketch in oval.

This Angel of the Presence and Chancellor of the heavens is also the Chief Recording Angel. With each of his seventy-two wings spanning the size of our world, this archangel is thought to be God's largest angel. Known as the angel of the face in sacred text, he is believed to have 365,000 eyes and an eternally burning flame for a body. This angel sits at the entrance of the Seventh heaven and is a member of the Serim.

CHAPTER 10

Archangel Michael

The Likeness of God

Archangel Michael whispers to you, "With just one call, the Angels of Mercy rush to your aid. Invite us into your life and we will remove your fears."

"Close your eyes and tell me which angel you see," I asked nine-year-old Riley.

"Why do I need to close my eyes?" he replied, pointing to the doorway leading out of his bedroom. "Two angels are standing right there!"

"Who are these angels?" I asked. Even though I couldn't see them, I had no doubt that Riley could.

"One is Michael and the other is ... um, I can't remember his name. He has orange hair and green clothes."

Riley told me that he always sees two angels standing in his doorway at night. I've learned not to question anything about angel sightings, especially when it includes powerful angels. From Riley's description, I had the feeling that Archangel Raphael was the one accompanying Michael in his doorway. It all made perfect sense. My first clue was that a lot of people report seeing Archangel Raphael's aura color as green and orange. An even bigger clue to the identity of this "mystery angel" was the archangel he was with. Archangel Michael has such a huge job of protecting the earth and all of its inhabitants, including you! Archangel Raphael likes to lend Michael a hand whenever possible.

Archangel Michael Versus the Devil

Artists who draw Michael often show him surrounded by white light and holding a big sword or staff. This is probably because many of the really old holy books, such as the Bible and the Koran, tell the story of Michael's fight against evil.

The story tells us that an angel named Beelzebub once had Archangel Michael's position as the top advisor to God. Thinking he was even more powerful than God, Beelzebub made some really poor choices. Acting like a big bully on a playground, Beelzebub ordered all of the other angels to either follow him or suffer!

When God found out what Beelzebub was doing, he became very sad. God asked him to leave heaven and take his followers with him. But like many bullies do, Beelzebub said, "Make me!"

In C. S. Lewis's *The Lion, The Witch, and The Wardrobe*, the mighty lion, Aslan, and his followers fight the evil witch and her gang. If you can imagine the battle in your mind's eye, you have a pretty good idea about what happened to Beelzebub and the angels who took his side.

God called on Michael to lead the battle against Beelzebub. Rounding up all of the angels who were still faithful to God's gentle ways, Archangel Michael asked them to help. On that day, the second best angel in heaven turned hero when Michael drew his mighty staff and tossed Beelzebub out. When that happened, God changed Beelzebub's name to Satan and called his band of followers "fallen angels." Having defeated the Devil and his forces, Michael took Beelzebub's place at God's right hand. Now as leader or "Chief of the Archangels," Michael is known as the "Angel who is like God."

Shield of Light

No matter who you are with, or where you are, you can call Michael's name, and he will cover you with the brilliance of his shield. Simply say, "Please, Archangel Michael, surround me with your light."

Even when you're afraid of something you can't explain or don't understand, you can call on Archangel Michael to shield you from fear of harm. Asking for Archangel Michael's help is not hard. Neither is trusting that he will take away your fears once you understand that the "Angel who is like God" is both powerful and loving. To build a trusting bond with Archangel Michael, make a list of whatever scares you.

For example, if somebody is causing you worry at school, add this person to your list. Draw a picture of yourself and then write the name of the scary person below it. You can sketch the person if you like. It doesn't have to look like the person in your mind as long as it serves as a symbol of your fear.

Using a light purple or sparkly white crayon, draw a circle around the sketch you have made of yourself. This is Archangel Michael's energy color, and it is your shield. As you draw the circle around yourself, say, "Archangel Michael, please break my connection to (the name of the item you have just circled), dissolve my fear, and protect me from harm."

Now, taking that same crayon, draw a circle around the person you have drawn who scares you. As you do this say, "Archangel Michael, please guide and protect (insert this person's name), and soften his heart."

Remember the story of Beelzebub and Michael? Like Satan, if a bully does not want to change his ways, Michael cannot interfere with his free will. But, as Michael helped the gentle, loving angels who wished to live peacefully in heaven, he can help you to live peacefully on earth.

Moving down your list, place a circle around yourself and each person or item with the same white or purple crayon. Don't forget to call on Archangel Michael each time you do this.

> *Archangel Michael, please break my connection to (the name of the item you have just circled), dissolve my fear, and protect me from harm. Archangel Michael, please guide and protect (insert this person's name), and soften his heart.*

When you are finished, take the paper, and rip or cut away each fearful word or picture, leaving only you on the paper. Now, tape the small piece of paper to a mirror or other place in your room where you can easily see it. Return to the image often, and each time you do, say, "Thank you, Michael, for protecting me and dissolving my fears."

Do this again tomorrow and for five more days. Each time, list or draw your fears. Take old ones off your list or include new ones as necessary.

Archangel Michael says, "Deciding to remove a fearful item means that fear is now gone!"

If a fear remains at the end of the five days, go outside and take a walk around your house or your backyard. Try to get alone so that you can have a one-to-one talk with Michael. You don't need to see him to talk to him, but if you are anything like Riley, you just might!

Ask Archangel Michael to help you further using these words:

If there is still something I am afraid of that I have not put on my list, please help me to know what it is and please dissolve this fear like you did the rest. Thank you, Archangel Michael, for taking away my fear.

Whatever pops into your mind is what you need to mentally cut away before your fear can go. It could be anything. Just trust that Michael is guiding you toward peace and joy. Archangel Michael asks that I remind you that placing his shield around your fear does no harm to the person or creature.

By asking for the protection of the angels, you move away from conflict toward peace—and so does the person or thing you are most afraid to face.

Remember to call on Archangel Michael anytime you feel you need protection. Think of this archangel as "My–call."

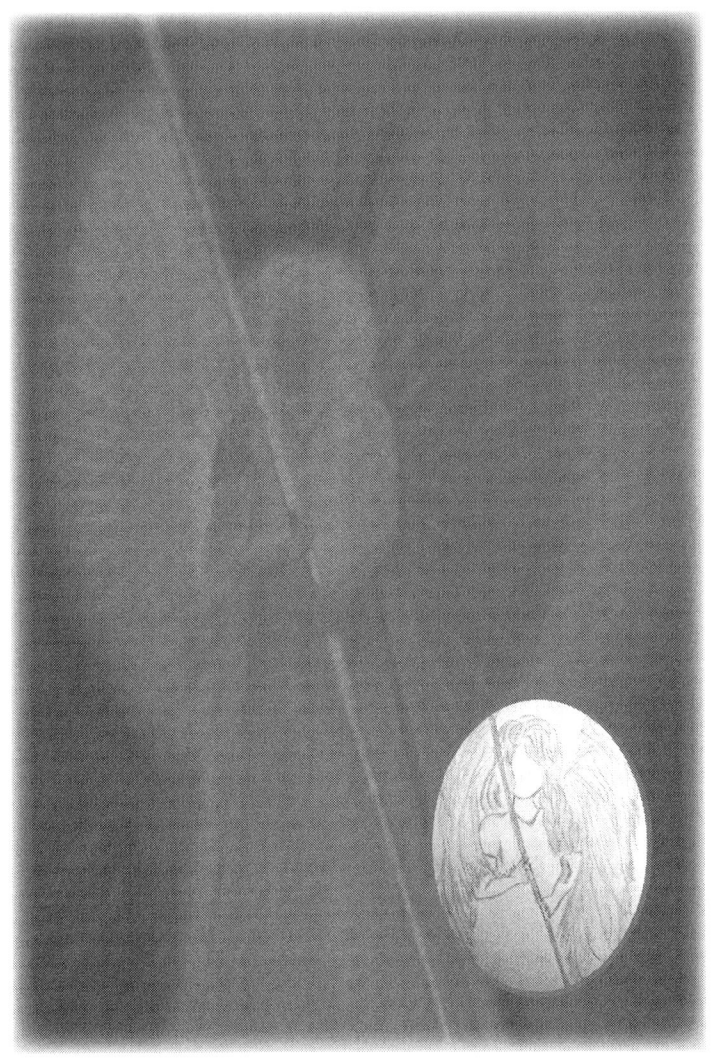

Archangel Michael with original sketch in oval.

This archangel is the Warrior of the Heavens, Ruler of the Archangels, Prince of the Presence, Chief of Virtues, Prince of Seraphim, and Angel of Mercy and Amends. He is the Defender of Chaos, Repentance, Righteousness, Truth, War, and, believe it or not, snow! This Ruler of the Sun is thought to be so much like God, that he is even said to have been the speaker in Moses' burning bush. Simply put, this Ally of Israel is considered to be the greatest angel in heaven.

CHAPTER 11

Archangel Raphael

God Heals

Archangel Raphael whispers to you, "Close your eyes sweet child and feel the comfort of our embrace. Wrap yourself in our healing light and know that we are with you always."

WHILE PLAYING, TWO BOYS stumbled on a nest of yellow jackets tucked behind storage boxes in a shed. As the bees emerged from their hive, one of the boys threw an empty can at the nest. Running out of the shed, he left his startled friend alone with a swarm of angry bees.

In a panic, the friend screamed and brushed the bees away. He too ran from the shed, but not before one very frightened yellow jacket plunged a stinger into his arm. Immediately, the arm began to swell. By the time he ran home to tell his mother what had happened, it was too late to remove the stinger.

That night, the boy snuggled under his covers to go to sleep. No matter how hard he tried to relax, his arm throbbed. Closing his eyes, he thought about Archangel Raphael. He imagined that Archangel Raphael had made himself as small as a mite.

"Archangel Raphael, please help my arm to feel better so that I can sleep, and could you please go under my skin and push the stinger up so that I can pull it out of me in the morning? Thank you for healing me, Raphael," the boy whispered. He knew the importance of always giving thanks for angel blessings.

As the boy began to relax, he imagined Archangel Raphael fluttering around in his arm. He could feel Raphael's soft velvety feathers tickling him just beneath the penetration point of the stinger as they brushed away the poison the bee had injected into his arm. He imagined the miniature version of Archangel Raphael soaring beneath the stinger and gently guiding it to the surface of his skin.

At some point during all that imagining, the boy fell into a deep sleep. When he woke the next morning, the pain in his arm was gone. Running his hand over the infected area, he felt something small poking through his skin. There, sticking out of the same place it had entered in the afternoon before was the stinger!

Archangel Raphael, the Healing Angel

The very thought of Archangel Raphael makes me smile. He is one of the kindest, most giving angels. He is also one of the easiest angels to get to know. Archangel Raphael loves people. Like an older brother or sister, he has a great sense of duty to watch over you at all times. His presence is the strongest of any of the angels. Whether you have called on him or not, Archangel Raphael stays by your side every day and each night while you sleep. His favorite thing in this world is to do a good deed for you.

Archangel Raphael can heal you and anyone else. But keep in mind, just as a doctor cannot touch your body without you or your parent's permission, neither can Raphael. In order for him to work his healing miracles, you have to invite him to help. You can even invite your parents to join in when you ask Raphael to bring his healing power into your life.

> *Dearest Archangel Raphael, please wrap my body with your healing green energy. With every breath I take, I feel your soothing powers working inside me to heal my wounds and quiet my pain.*

Like the boy in our story, you may wish to state specifically what you would like healed, such as a bee sting or a sore throat.

Not so long ago, a friend of mine was in the hospital suffering from an infection. After a painful series of nerve operations on a badly cut arm, Devon was admitted to the hospital after the doctors discovered his body was filling with a poisonous infection.

The night he was hospitalized, I spoke with Archangel Raphael.

Dearest Raphael, thank you so much for being with Devon through each of his surgeries. Thank you for saving his life the night of his accident. Thank you for empowering him to use his right arm again. Now that he is healing, I ask you to please stay by his side. Please wrap him in your healing green light. Breathe your spirit into Devon to dissolve the poison that has taken over his body so that he may be strong and filled with light and energy once again.

Before I asked Archangel Raphael to help my friend, I made a point to thank Raphael for all he had done for me in the past before asking for specific help with this new health problem. After speaking with Raphael, I told Devon that Archangel Raphael wished to know exactly where he hurt, so he could help the pain to go away faster. God gave free will to everybody. No person or angel can mess with a human's free will. This means that it was Devon's job to ask Raphael and his Band of Mercy to help before they could do what I had asked them to do for him. By mentioning Archangel Raphael to Devon, I planted the idea of Raphael's healing power in his mind. This way, even if Devon didn't believe in the power of the angels, he might ask Archangel Raphael for healing help when he was alone and quiet in his hospital room.

Thoughts are very powerful. With angels now in Devon's thoughts, the chances of him asking Archangel Raphael for help had greatly improved. Angels can't mess with free will, but they are wise—and they can be very tricky!

Many people who have experienced great pain in their lives are quick to call on Raphael for aid. Other people believe only a doctor can make them feel better.

Archangel Raphael says, "You must place your belief in your doctors and nurses. They are God's healers on the earth. Our job is simply to assist them in their healing. When your physical form is unwell, your spirit is in need of pure love. That is where we come in. Your doctors and nurses care for your body, and the angels care for your spirit."

The Traveler

In the ancient books, Archangel Raphael meets a traveler named Tobias and the woman he loves. Archangel Raphael is pretending to be another traveler when they meet. Tobias has no idea he is in the company of an angel and invites Raphael to join him on his journey. Along the way, Raphael learns that the woman Tobias loves is too sick for Tobias to marry. This sly archangel, disguised as a traveler, cures the woman so that Tobias and his love can be married.

Impressed by Raphael's kindness, Tobias invites the stranger home. When they arrive, Tobias eagerly introduces Archangel Raphael to his blind father, Tobit. Straight away, Raphael placed mud in the blind man's eyes and laid his hands on his body.

"Wash the mud away and your eyes will be opened," Archangel Raphael said.

At once, Tobit's eyes were opened. Seeing Archangel Raphael for who he was, Tobit knew he was in the company of an angel.

This story tells us about Raphael's healing powers. It also explains why this angel known as "God heals" is considered the angel of safe travel. Working with Archangel Michael, these two mighty archangels guide us in our travels. Now that you know this, the next time you are going to a faraway place or even someplace close to home, call on Archangel Raphael to help you get to where you are going easily.

The Sign Game

Archangel Raphael says, "You will find us hiding along your way. We are on billboards, in tunnels, and in the clouds. You might even hear our message on another's lips. Is it intended for you? Watch, listen, and be open to what is in front of your nose. Come, let's play a game of hide and seek! Can you hear the angels' secret language? Can you spot the angels' signs? Watch for us. Listen for our whispers. We are right here, by your side."

Before beginning your trip simply say:

> *Archangel Raphael, thank you for watching out for me always. Thank you for healing my pain and guiding me on my journeys.*

Could you please clear the road I travel and help this trip to be enjoyable for everyone else who is traveling too? Please stay with me to help me find fun and interesting stops along the way! Please, Archangel Raphael, show me signs that you are with me along the way.

Archangel Raphael loves this game! Even if you are taking a bus, a train, or an airplane, you can ask Raphael for a calm, relaxing trip—or to help you find an interesting person to help you pass the time while you travel.

Raphael will rush to your side the moment you call his name. You don't have to say it aloud; the thought of Archangel Raphael will pull his healing company close to you. Raphael will help your wounds heal and will get you to where you are going safely. His gentle touch can instantly relieve painful injuries and leave you feeling calm, at peace, and filled with the wisdom that you are never alone.

Close to dinnertime one evening soon after I finished typing these words, Raphael decided to send his message of never being alone to me. I had to make a quick trip to the grocery store around the corner. While rushing through the aisles and paying for my food, I continued to think about Archangel Raphael. When I got into my car, a song on the radio grabbed my attention. I had never heard it before, but I liked its melody and immediately began humming the tune. As I pulled out of the grocery store parking lot, the singer began singing. The first words I heard were: "I love my angels, and I know they love me!"

"Thank you, Raphael!" I laughed. This song was a gentle reminder that Raphael and his Band of Mercy are always with me—even during the shortest of trips.

Ask what you need from this generous angel. And then, please, don't forget to thank him for his help. Remember, gratitude is very important when dealing with the angels. Archangel Raphael says, "It works very well with humans too!"

When you go someplace strange, or need a hand to feel well, like a "raft" in a watery storm, Archangel Raphael will propel you forward!

Archangel Raphael with original sketch in oval

This Ruler of the second heaven is Regent of the Sun, Chief of the Virtues, and Head of the Guardian Angels. As the Angel of Healing and Science, this powerful archangel has been called the Angel of Knowledge. This most loved archangel is a member of the Seraphim, the Dominions and the Cherubim, and the Defender of Compassion, Healing, Love, Progress, and Repentance.

CHAPTER 12

Archangel Raguel

God Heals

Archangel Raguel whispers to you, "We see your weaknesses dear child. We hear you crying in the night. And we love you! We see your strengths dear child. We hear your laughter in the wind. And still we love you. We see your humanity dear child. We know your spirit. And Yes! We love you."

YOU HAVE PROBABLY HEARD a lot about heaven in your lifetime. I'm sure you've even formed a few ideas of your own. Archangel Raguel is said to be the angel who reviews your life's purpose after your spirit leaves this earth and decides where it will go from here. Many people believe if you make a great many mistakes on earth, your spirit will suffer after death.

I think this is a sad point of view. Happily, so do a great many others! These people believe the universe, or God, is our creator and see God as a heavenly blend of the perfect parent.

Imagine what it would be like if you took the personalities of all those people who love and care for you and mixed them all together to make one person! Would this new person be funny and strict? Would you have created an interesting combination of playful and calm? Or would this blend make someone who is forgiving and demanding? Either way, this person would love you just because you are.

If you have a good relationship with those who take care of you, you will understand how limitless God's love can be. But if your relationships are not so good, trust me when I say this in no way affects how God and the angels see you.

God created you exactly as you are. God has complete love for your spirit as well as all those fascinating behaviors that make you human! As infinite as the universe, so is God's love for you. In fact, God loves you so much that he has assigned his best friend, Archangel Raguel, to welcome your spirit back into the heavens when your body is no longer needed.

The Mystifying Archangel Raguel

Ancient stories tell us Archangel Raguel is one of the angels who sit closest to God in heaven. Do you believe there is an angel who judges our actions and thoughts? Do you think this angel will punish you for the things you think you have done badly or the people you have hurt in your lifetime? If you've said yes to either of these questions, without a doubt Archangel Raguel is the angel you are thinking of.

Do you believe there is a place in heaven for those who do good deeds on earth? Do you think there is another place, somewhere outside of heaven, for those who are cruel? If you do, then the horrible job of assigning which place you will go would also fall to Archangel Raguel.

If this idea of the afterlife is true, Archangel Raguel is the only angel I have ever known to be cruel and unforgiving. Considering all this, at first I was afraid to read about Raguel. I mean, who wants to draw their attention to a spiteful angel? There was no way I wanted to mess with that!

I made quite an effort to learn about Archangel Raguel, but nothing I read about him made sense to me. How could God, who loves us so much, force you or any of his children to suffer punishment from a mean and unforgiving angel?

I thought about the naughty things I had done when I was a little girl. I called my grandfather plump. I wished my sister belonged to another family. Once, I even stole a pair of earrings! Would I be judged on the things I did when I was five, ten, or thirteen? I can't imagine a loving parent holding a grudge for an entire lifetime. What seemed even stranger to me was the idea of my father asking a family friend to decide the proper punishment for my deeds.

Finally, he came to visit me one morning! What I thought was the light of daybreak spreading over me turned out to be Archangel Raguel's soft, tender aura. Opening my eyes, I felt an incredible friendliness fill my heart. Archangel Raguel's light was fleeting, but his message was clear.

God is love, he told me. In that moment I completely understood Raguel's position in heaven.

That morning, and for many days after, I spoke with Archangel Raguel about his purpose. I also read and reread all I could find on this most compassionate of angels. I discovered that Archangel Raguel is far from being the horrifying angel described in ancient books. Known as the "Friend of God," Archangel Raguel is the archangel of openness and fair dealings.

Archangel Raguel's Message for You

Archangel Raguel wants you to know that God only wants the best for you. He understands you even better than your family or your friends—and he would never bring harm to you as a means of punishment.

> "It is my job to gently show you the error of your ways when you have done something you know is wrong. It is my job to help you to overcome your difficulties. Allow me—and my choir of angels—to put you back on the right track. We will steer you in the right direction and let your free will guide you to make the best decisions."

Get to Know Archangel Raguel

Raguel came to me with compassion and love. Just as your parent would ask a close family friend to show you the way to or from school or meet you at soccer practice, God sends Archangel Raguel to kindly guide you along your path. Along with Jeremiel and Azrael, Archangel

Raguel and his choir of angels show your spirit how to get to heaven; once you arrive, they welcome you home.

If you think that you have done something awful in your life, Archangel Raguel is the friend you need to call upon. When I was five and told my grandpa he was plump, I didn't understand how my words would have hurt his feelings. When I was ten and wished my sister could live with another family, I didn't realize how much I needed her in my life. When I was thirteen and figured I didn't need to pay for what I wanted, I had no idea how my actions could bring loss to my favorite store. Worse still, I wasn't able to predict how the shame of stealing would change the positive view I had of myself.

Now it's your turn. Imagine you are a hotshot photojournalist like Jimmy Olsen from the Superman comic books. As Clark Kent's sidekick, Jimmy took pictures of life. With Archangel Raguel as the superhero in your life, your mission, if you choose to accept it, is to take photographs of every meaningful event in your life. Grab your camera and start taking control of the world around you!

Print the pictures that capture the most meaningful events for you. Put them together into a private newspaper of your life. You can use newsprint, a scrapbook, or an old notebook from school. Whatever way you choose to make your newspaper, remember to include a headline for every entry you make.

In my newspaper, I would include a picture of my Grandpa laughing, with a headline reading, "Words Have Power!" Over a photo of my sister and I hugging, my headline might read, "Much Loved, Much Needed." And over a picture of a pair of earrings, the headline could read, "Bad Decisions Do Not Make Bad People!"

Don't forget to include the happy events in your life right alongside the not-so-happy ones. For example, when I was five, I loved visiting my grandparents. Beside the photo of my grandfather, I might include another photo of the two of us cuddling. I bet you have a great idea for that headline! Beside my sister's picture, I might include a picture of us having a candy picnic in our bedroom. I'm sure you get the point.

In making a newspaper of your life, you'll have a permanent record of your good will and kindness toward others during those times in your life when everything you do feels like a mistake.

Calling on Archangel Raguel

Archangel Raguel wants you to know that for every mistake you make, he sees at least ten of your good deeds. "When you feel the need to talk about your actions, please call on us!"

You can start simply by saying:

> *Archangel Raguel, thank you for hearing my words. I have (Insert the action you thought was wrong). I realize this was hurtful for everyone involved and ask your guidance in putting this behind me, and changing my ways so that I treat myself and others with respect now and always. Thank you.*

Archangel Raguel says, "We are your friends. Our job is to watch over you at all times, to set you on your path, to help you discover your wings! Hold onto your mistakes, and you will never allow yourself the freedom to find the love that awaits you in heaven. Forgive yourself and others and draw ever closer to 'The Light.' See your own greatness!"

> *Archangel Rag-uel urges you to get rid of your past wrongs the same way you would get rid of old rags. Toss them away!*

Archangel Raguel with original sketch in oval

In charge of the second heaven, this Ruler of the Dominions is a member of the Sarim and an Angel of the Presence.

CHAPTER 13

Archangel Raziel

Secret of God

> *Archangel Raziel whispers to you, "God's secret is inside of you. His mystery is a simple puzzle. To understand you are one with the universe is to achieve your heart's desire."*

Have you ever noticed how the light catches something just the right way and creates a rainbow of color? A sudden move or blink and the colors disappear. Well, that sort of describes what it is like to find this next archangel. For those of you who enjoy a good hunt, strap on your headlamps and pull on your hiking boots. We are going to the highest point in heaven to find this clever archangel!

Just as the sunshine creates a rainbow after a summer shower, Archangel Raziel carries such a bright light that it spreads open into a rainbow of color whenever he is near. This breaking of light is the consequence of what scientists call refraction, or a prism effect.

Angel watchers also see the rainbow as a special sign. It is the sign of "The Secret of God." While many of the most powerful angels radiate one or two auras, or a misty color, Archangel Raziel outshines them all with every color of the rainbow. The next time you look into the sky and see a rainbow, smile because Archangel Raziel is near.

Who is Archangel Raziel?

Considered to be the oldest of all archangels, Raziel is most definitely the smartest. And he has the coolest job! As the "Guardian of the Mystery," it is Archangel Raziel's mission to guard God's image from the world. With only the sheerness of a curtain to separate them, Archangel Raziel hears all of God's secrets!

When the very first man and woman roamed the earth, Archangel Raziel decided to gather all he knew and put it into a book called *The Book of Raziel*. At that time, Adam and Eve lived in a beautiful garden created by God. This was a very special place where the people lived in harmony with the beasts. Even the snakes had legs, and they could talk!

In the middle of the garden stood the Tree of Life. This tree was the only thing that God asked those living there not to touch. One day while wandering in the garden, a snake met Eve along her path. As they neared the Tree of Life, the snake suggested that Eve pluck an apple and eat it.

"No!" gasped Eve. "It is the Lord's Tree."

"All of God's secrets are contained in the fruit of that tree," the snake laughed. "If you eat the fruit, you will be like God."

Eve could not believe her ears. Could this be true? Could eating from the Tree of Life really be all she needed to do to be just like God?

Eve chose to believe the snake's trickery rather than simply enjoying the gifts God had given her. Being afraid to do this alone, Eve brought Adam with her to the tree. Telling him about her encounter with the snake, she convinced Adam to pluck a ripe red apple from the tree.

As soon as they bit into an apple, Adam and Eve were filled with shame. To worsen their troubles, when asked if they had eaten from God's tree, they each blamed the other for breaking the rules. Adam and Eve felt embarrassed by their actions. At once, they decided they could no longer live in God's garden. Hopeful that God's children would one day return to the garden, Archangel Raziel gave Enoch, Adam, and Eve's grandchild his book of knowledge (See Chapter 9).

Archangel Raziel understands how easy it can be to slip. He reminds you that, as a human being living on this earth, you will make mistakes in your lifetime. Understanding God will seem nearly impossible when you choose to listen only to your human side. Like

Adam and Eve, you may even believe you are not good enough to ask for help from God or the angels.

Archangel Raziel says, "That is just not true!"

When you try to only show people your spiritual side, you might find yourself forgetting to be grateful for all the incredible things this earth has to offer. To really understand God's mysteries, you need to discover your special human qualities and your spirit's reason for being here.

Archangel Raziel says, "Open your eyes to infinite love. The mystery of God is within you. Like Adam and Eve, you were fashioned to be as one with all!"

Could it be because of Raziel's book that Adam and Eve's family was able to survive outside of the garden? From the first two people to ever walk the earth, Adam and Eve went on to create such an enormous family that every person on this earth is believed to be a great-, great-, great- … great-grandchild of Adam and Eve. Including you!

Archangel Raziel's Challenge to You

Besides giving away his most precious secrets, Archangel Raziel watches over each of us from his throne in the heavens. Your body grows bigger and your mind stronger while Archangel Raziel whispers the mysteries of heaven in your ear. For those adventurers who truly wish to see the wisest of angels, Raziel offers this challenge: Spend a day walking in another's shoes.

Pretend you are your pet dog or cat and walk around on your hands and knees. Ask your mother if you can try eating your food with no hands and lap water from a bowl. Don't eat off of the floor or from your pet's bowl, but you may like to give it a try from your own bowl at your kitchen table.

Maybe you could try living in your brother or sister's shoes. Ask to switch rooms, toys, and friends for a day! Or maybe you could be one of your parents for the day. Try cleaning the house and preparing the family meals. Get your family organized for a fun-filled day together. Why not come up with a few ideas of your own?

If you are old enough to volunteer, ask to help out at a local kennel, hospital, or senior's home. Spend a dinner hour helping out at a soup kitchen—or an afternoon collecting clothes and spare household items for the needy.

Ask your parents if they know of a neighbor who could use a hand mowing the lawn or cleaning out a room in the house? Why not spend a morning with that person? Ask about the pictures hanging in her front hall. Fix him a cup of tea or a sandwich, and visit, just visit.

What can you learn from another person? Challenge yourself. The list of how you can "walk in another's shoes" is endless, but if the thoughts of helping another seem more like chore than a fun way to spend your day, ask Archangel Raziel to help you see the real value of what you are about to do.

Asking for Raziel's Guidance

> *Archangel Raziel, thank you for guiding me to see what is really important in my life. Thank you for helping me to understand others. For just (insert the amount of time you would like to walk in another's shoes) lead me to the right place where I can be of most value to another as well as myself, so that this action might bring about the highest good for all. Thank you for staying with me and helping me enjoy this opportunity.*

Archangel Raziel Wants you to know that you have the power of the angels inside of you. You can learn the secrets of the universe. You are your own rainbow.

This wise old archangel brings to you the colorful, dazzling rays of the sun. Archangel Raziel is your razzle-dazzle angel!

Archangel Raziel with original sketch in oval

Regarded as the most knowledgeable, this magical archangel is a member of the Cherubim, Guardian of the Mystery, and Prince of the ancient Order of Erelim. Erelim is a very old name for the heavenly choir called Thrones. See Chapter 17, Society of Divine Beings.

CHAPTER 14

Archangel Sandalphon

The Messenger of God

> *Archangel Sandalphon whispers to you, "My choir of angels and I are here to help you reach out to God. It is easy! Give thanks for what you have. Be loving to everyone you meet. Tell God what is most important to you. God gets every one of your prayers. You need only listen to your heart for God's answer."*

WHEN YOU WERE BORN, at least one angel was assigned to sit on either side of your new human body. These angels are guardians who stay with you during your life. Whispering heavenly guidance in your ear, they lead you through your life on earth. These angels stay beside you from birth until the day the body dies and your spirit returns to its home in heaven. Forever caring for your spirit, these loving angels stay with you even after the body is gone.

As "Chief of the Guardian Angels," it is Archangel Sandalphon's pleasure to guide you through your life. Rushing to your side from the moment you were born, Sandalphon lovingly steers you in the right direction.

I first learned about Sandalphon when I decided it was time to get to know my guardian angel. I closed my eyes, breathed deeply, and counted. In my mind's eye, I could see myself walking down a spiral set of stairs toward a bright light. With each number I counted and each breath I took, I felt myself getting closer to the light. By the time I reached the number twelve, the light was all around me. Standing in front of me, slightly to my right, I saw what appeared to be a nine-year-old girl.

"Who are you?" I asked.

"I am Matilda!" she stated. Her voice was a sweet whisper. She spoke to me about my body and my spirit. She reminded me that there are many, many souls who love me on this earth and in heaven.

Early in the morning, when the house is still very quiet, I sit in the same place as I did on the day that I first met Matilda. I want to see her kind, round face. I long to look into her soft green eyes. Every day, I call on her to visit. Day after day, Matilda complies.

"We are happy to see you. How can we help?" she asked.

She says *we*, but there is only *her*. At first, I wondered why she said *we* when I thought she should have been saying *I*. When I asked Matilda about this, she giggled and gently shook her head. It was as though she had not understood my question.

As her visits became a regular part of my mornings, I had the unmistakable feeling that there was at least one more angel present in the room besides Matilda. Some days, it felt as if the entire room was filled with angels! I simply could not shake off the feeling that an extremely powerful angel accompanied her when she appeared to me each day.

Two weeks into our daily meetings, I finally asked Matilda directly, "Is there another angel with you?"

"Well, of course!" she answered playfully. "Can you not see?"

"No. Where is this angel?"

"Everywhere!"

The sound of Matilda's giggles calmed my mind and lightened my heart. It was as if my eyes had been closed and were now opened. All at once, I was able to see what was right there in front and all around me. The bright yellow light emanating from behind Matilda came from a surprisingly tall angel.

It was Archangel Sandalphon! Except maybe for his twin, Archangel Metatron (See Chapter 9), Archangel Sandalphon stood taller and brighter than any other angel I had ever met.

God's Postman

In life, Metatron was Enoch—and his brother was Elijah. When it was time for the brothers to leave the earth, Enoch was lifted to the heavens by the archangels. Elijah was carried to heaven in a fiery chariot. Once there, God transformed him into Archangel Sandalphon, making Elijah the second human ever to become an angel.

While he lived as a human being on this earth, Elijah was a great prophet. In other words, he would speak to God for those people who believed they could not speak to God themselves. On the day of his transformation, Elijah became Sandalphon, God's personal postman. Working with Metatron, Sandalphon upholds his position as "Brother to the Message of God."

Archangel Sandalphon is said to stand so tall that he can touch heaven from earth. Reaching down to collect your earthly prayers, Sandalphon lifts them to heaven. Linking them together as one, Sandalphon presents your chain of devotions to God. Working in harmony, Metatron records God's response and hands it back to Sandalphon who delivers it to you.

The Presence of God

Like his brother, this Angel of the Presence reminds you that it is natural for your spirit to be surrounded by angels.

I call upon my guardian angels day after day. Like old friends, Sandalphon and Matilda always know what is in my heart. Because of this, I no longer need to do a great deal of talking. Visiting with them has become my time to listen. I just close my eyes, take three or four belly breaths, and relax. This is my time to listen to my personal messages from the angels.

Many people who have been raised with the Eastern Hindu, Buddhist, or Baha'i faith believe a spirit can return to earth to live a second, third, or even fourth human life. It is the duty of our heavenly guardians to help each spirit decide to remain in heaven or live another human life on earth.

Like Archangel Sandalphon, you are a messenger of God. As an angel-force on this earth, you carry God's promise in your prayers. They are powerful!

Talking to God

Talking to God is like talking to the person who loves you the most in the world. Archangel Sandalphon asks you to use your power often to help yourself and others.

Archangel Sandalphon says, "Prayer is simple. Prayer is easy. Prayer is fun. Find a quiet place and close your eyes. Now just talk to God. Say whatever you want to say. When you are sick, talk to God. When you are healthy, talk to God. When you are fearful, talk to God. When you are happy, talk to God."

Archangel Sandalphon's Simple Prayer

A simple prayer to God is a miracle you have created! Just breathe in the fresh air of the universe and speak in simple words. If you are not sure how to begin, try using this prayer until you feel comfortable saying prayers of your own:

> *Dear God in heaven, thank you for opening my heart to your love. Thank you for the signs and songs of the angels. Alone, I am afraid, but as one with all your creations, I know that I am safe. I thank you for being with (use name of person you are praying for). With your guidance, I know that out of this (illness, disaster, fear), something truly wonderful is on its way.*

"Say what is in your heart," advises Archangel Sandalphon. "God gives gifts for the spirit, not for the body. Give thanks. Send love. Be happy. This is how you will become closer to God."

Remember as an earth angel, Archangel "Sand'al'phon" is your warm, sandy-yellow "tele-phone" line to God.

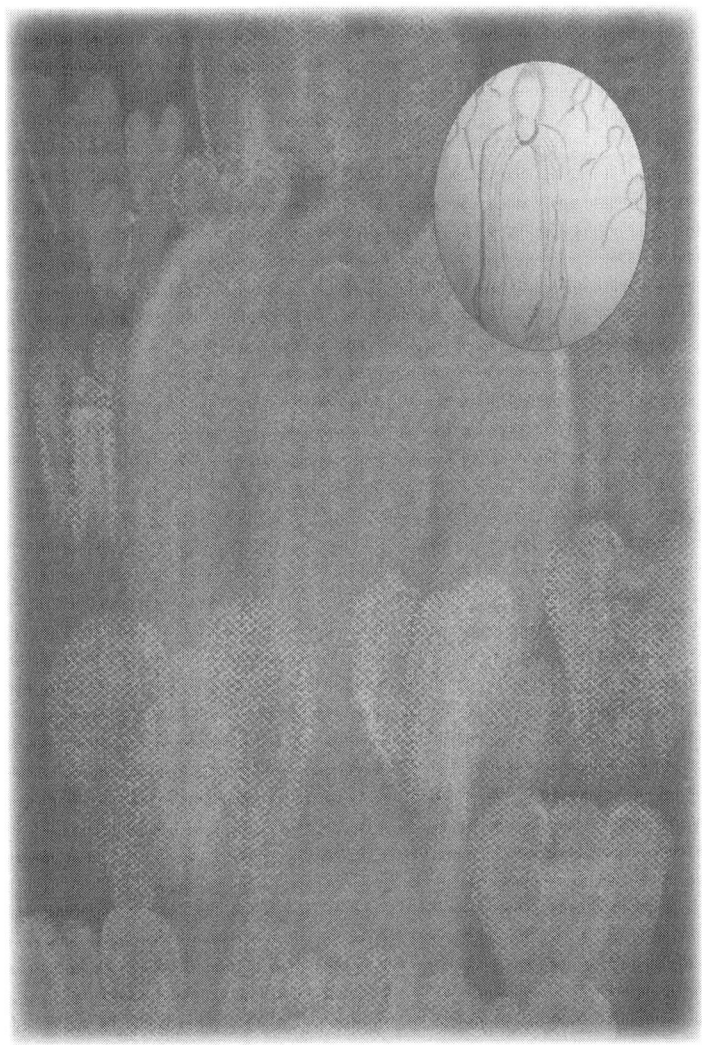

Archangel Sandalphon and his Guardian Angels with original in oval

This "Angel of the Presence" is also the Head of the Guardian Angels and Defender of Embryo, Glory, and Tears.

CHAPTER 15

Archangel Uriel

The Fire of God

Archangel Uriel whispers to you, Feel the fire of God in your heart. Fill yourself up with the wonders of the universe. Love the gift of you.

WHEN I WAS NINE years old, I told my mother that I was going to move away. I didn't like her rules anymore, and I thought I could live a better life outside of her home. I packed a small bag and told her I was leaving. Recognizing my suitcase as the one I kept my Barbie dolls in, my mother smiled and told me to have a safe trip.

I was enraged! Not getting the response I had wished for, I stormed back into my room and slammed the door with a resounding bang. "You are not my mother anymore!" I yelled. "I hate you!"

Tears stung my eyes, and fire rose in my cheeks. How could I have been so mean to my own mom?

It has always been easy for me to talk with God. On this day, he seemed even more approachable than my mother did. Knowing that I had hurt her with my words and actions, I wondered if there really was a fiery place called hell. If there was such a place, I was certain I'd be going there. My only chance for escape was to request forgiveness!

"Please God!" I gasped between tearful hiccups. "Forgive me!"

His response came to me as a thought. God sent Archangel Uriel to whisper, "Your cruel behavior is not for God to forgive. In his eyes, you are always light. You are always love. It is your earth mother who needs to hear what is truly in your heart."

Uriel's Key to Hell

In cartoons and horror movies, hell is a fiery place located somewhere below the earth. This home of Satan is thought to be where wrongdoers go instead of heaven. Those who must go there are believed to be greeted by Satan. His job is to torture the souls who have not followed God's rules. Pretty scary place, huh?

Some of these old stories go on to say that Archangel Uriel holds the key to a fear-riddled place called hell. Considered Regent of the Sun and Defender of Thunder, it is a long-held belief that this wily archangel uses severe weather conditions to scare innocents away from the gates of hell.

For centuries, this idea of hell has taught children and adults to fear God. But Archangel Uriel and his band of mercy tell us that hell may not be a place at all. In fact, as God's children, we have free will to decide if we choose to believe in actual places called heaven or hell.

Could it be possible that heaven and hell exist right here on earth? Archangel Uriel urges you to use your powerful mind to decide what you truly believe. If the angels are part of us, couldn't heaven and hell be a part of us as well?

Think back to a time when you laughed and played with a close friend or a loving parent. Think back to the best time you've ever had. Close your eyes and ask Archangel Uriel to take you there again. How do you feel? Could you get any happier than you are at this very moment? Is it possible that you have just experienced a little piece of heaven?

Now close your eyes again and think back to a time when you were very mad. Where were you? Who was with you? What made you so mad?

Feel your heart beating. Hear yourself breathing. Feel the tears sting your eyes. Is your skin hot?

If heaven and hell are not places outside of this world, they might just be inventions of your mind. If that's true, could anger be your own little piece of hell? Does thinking about being angry make you angry? Is that your hell?

Even at nine, the moment the words, "I hate you!" left my lips, I knew what it was like to be in hell. My mother loved me so much, and I had broken her heart.

Archangel Uriel says, "Fear and sadness are the only keys to hell. To hold them is to find yourself locked behind iron gates you alone have built. Call on my angels of mercy to help you to reinvent your own version of heaven. When you do this, you will have put hell behind you forever!"

Archangel Uriel on Finding Heaven

To forever live in heaven, you must come to know your happy self. The easiest way to do this is to use your incredible mind.

Have you ever had a school project that just seemed too hard to get done? Did your mom ever ask you a question that made your mind feel full of cotton? Has your dad ever asked for help to fix something—and you just didn't know what to do? Me too!

Archangel Uriel wants you to know that you are a child of God. Your spirit has taken human form for the purpose of making mistakes! That's how you learn.

Archangel Uriel is a friendly teacher, searching for the best way to help you learn. And like a caring teacher, Archangel Uriel shows his thundery side as well as his warm, sunny side. He knows everything there is to know about the universe, and his job is to share it with us! Known as the "Fire of God," or "God Light," this tall, majestic angel will rush to your side whenever you are in doubt.

"Call on us angels to help you study for a test or when you are unsure about answering a school question. Call on us for understanding when you feel like you have none. Use the amazing power of your mind. By understanding yourself, you understand your world. Teach others to do the same."

Bringing Archangel Uriel into Your Life

Archangel Uriel wants you to call on him to better understand who you are and what you can do to make the world a better place for all. Change must start with you for the world to become balanced.

Archangel Uriel wishes you to know that everyone on this earth has God's gifts available to them. By your actions and words, you can help others find their inner heaven by seeing their own happiness.

With these simple words, Archangel Uriel can help you to become closer to God:

> *Thank you, Archangel Uriel, for giving me the power to expand my mind. Please help me understand my world and all of the people I share it with.*

To bring Archangel Uriel into your life, challenge yourself to have better understanding of your world by challenging your mind. Break out your old puzzles or search for tongue twister books at the library. Stretch your mind by reading adventurous books and finding inspiring hobbies. Study a new language. Learn to knit! Archangel Uriel finds joy in anything that keeps your mind busy.

Go one step further by learning about ways to weather cycles that affect our earth. Or, if you prefer, just look for cycles that affect your own life. Make up a "Happiness Game." Challenge your friends to think of all the times they have really felt happy and include them in your game.

Make weather cards that show various patterns. Play a flashcard game with your cards. Challenge others to find a happy message in each turned card—no matter the weather pattern.

Ask yourself about your "Happiness Game." *Is my game going to be funny? Or is it just going to be a lot of fun?*

Archangel Uriel wants you to challenge yourself. Trust in yourself, and use your skills to make a difference. It really doesn't matter what you do—just remember to invite Archangel Uriel along!

Archangel Uriel says, "We angels stand before the gates of heaven. Come to us with the fire of God in your heart, and you will forever find peace."

Strong as a "rail", quick as lightning, fire-angel U'riel" reminds you to look within to find your true power.

Archangel Uriel with original in oval

Not surprisingly this Angel of the Presence, Member of the Cherubim and Seraphim, Regent of the Sun, and Defender of Music, Poetry, Repentance, and Thunder is in charge of the weather. As the Angel of Prophecy, he holds a book and scroll in one hand and an open flame signifying God in the other. As the cherub who guards the entrance to the Garden of Eden, his flame is often within a sword.

CHAPTER 16

Archangel Zadkiel

Righteousness of God

> *Archangel Zadkiel whispers to you, "When you feel alone, be willing to follow your heart."*

Do you ever feel misunderstood? Do you ever feel like nobody will ever or could ever appreciate you? Do you ever wonder if you even understand yourself? If so, Archangel Zadkiel can help.

Archangel Zadkiel visited me as I woke up from an unforgettable dream. I knew I had been sent a heavenly message, but I wasn't really sure what it meant. In the dream, everyone around me—including my closest friends and family members—was rehearsing for a play. I was very ill and could not make any of them believe it. They all insisted I join them or be an outsider. Only my very best friend knew how sick I was. Like me, he was faced with laughter and disbelief every time he tried to tell the rest that I really was too sick to join their game.

In time, a little girl approached and asked me to rehearse with her. In her excitement, she jumped up off of the floor, caught me around the neck, and wrapped her legs around my waist. I was too weak to hold her weight and together we fell to the floor.

"You did that on purpose!" she cried.

Right away, I was surrounded by a group of angry people accusing me of hurting the little girl. I was very dizzy, and I found it hard to breathe. Pushing back the crowd, my friend picked me up and carried me out of the angry mob. My family and friends had deserted me. I was on the outside.

I opened my eyes, still feeling badly about the dream. That's when I noticed a shape of white light standing beside my bed. Though I could not see a face, I knew this was a strong and determined angel with purpose. A very clear aura of purple and red emanated from his wings.

"When you feel alone in this world, we are here to help," Archangel Zadkiel whispered.

Known as the "Righteousness of God," this angel of communication can fix misunderstandings between yourself and others. Like an angelic shield, Archangel Zadkiel fends off hurt feelings and helps you think about yourself confidently.

If life was a soccer game, Archangel Zadkiel would be your own private defenseman. He clears the way so that you can deflect those who might steal the ball. With Archangel Zadkiel on your side, you will make it successfully to the goal line.

Archangel Zadkiel helps you better understand your friends and your family. He says, "You don't have to allow others to hurt you so you can keep them as friends. Love your friends without judging their actions, holding a grudge, or feeling hurt. We will help you to allow them to be who they are—without changing who you are."

Even when you don't feel as though you are being treated well, Archangel Zadkiel will help you overlook the actions of others and feel the love that is in your heart for them. To find Archangel Zadkiel, get on your feet. Get moving and get involved. Join your school basketball, soccer, or football team. Join a community bowling league or volunteer group. Become a scout or take part in the debate club.

No matter what your sport, find a way to become part of a team. Learn what it is like to count on others and have them count on you. By doing this, you will easily see Archangel Zadkiel everywhere you look. He will be the smile on your teammate's face. He will be the proud look in your dad's eyes. He will be the person who says, "Thanks for all you do."

For those of you who are part of a team and still don't feel as though you know Archangel Zadkiel, simply call on him. During a practice or just before the big game, invite Archangel Zadkiel to play along beside you. You can use these words until you feel confident enough to come up with your own:

Dearest Archangel Zadkiel, thank you for helping me to be such a successful (insert your role, or position here: defenseman, runner, swimmer, student, daughter, and so on). Today, and every day, I call on you to guide me in this game, as well as in my game of life. Help me see the ways I can be the best team player possible so as to bring about the best outcome for all involved. Thank you for staying by my side, now and forever.

Whether you are kicking the ball five yards closer to the goalpost or helping your reading buddy in the classroom doesn't matter to Archangel Zadkiel. He will help you to be more aware of the game you are playing and how best to assist those around you. When you need Archangel Zadkiel's help to talk with someone special, he will rush to your side to ensure your talk brings a shared appreciation for one another.

Archangel Zadkiel says, "Our guiding signs are all around you. Watch for them, make use of them, and find your bliss in each touchdown."

You'll never be "sad," when you remember that Archangel "Zad"-"kie"l holds the "key" to belonging.

Archangel Zadkiel with original in oval

As Ruler of the fifth heaven and Chief of the Dominions, this archangel is a planetary angel and the Ruler of Jupiter. The Defender of Memory and Justice, he is thought to have been the angel who saved Isaac from becoming Abraham's sacrifice.

CHAPTER 17

A Final Word

Imagine

EVERY PERSON WHO HAS ever lived breathes the same air you are breathing now. Katy Perry watches the masses draw near her stage in the same way Terry Fox saw people gather at the roadside to witness his historic marathon. Lady Diana smelled the flowers of her large cascading bouquet in the same way her daughter-in-law Kate would have smelled them on her wedding day. When Michael Phelps swims, he tastes the same cool water as Benjamin Franklin did during his famous swims. And just as Amelia Earhart would have felt the warmth of the afternoon sun as it hit her flight jacket, the great Dalai Lama's forehead beads under its heat.

Today, when you hear the sweet song of the robin redbreast, remember that all of these historic people once listened to the calming sound of the birds in the trees. Though they are no longer with us, they experienced the same experiences. They walked the same ground we now walk on. They enjoyed the same sun we enjoy and shared the air as we now do. They were once part of our society. In this way, our shared experiences help us recognize a part of them in ourselves.

Another experience you share is the deep knowing that there is something more to our world than the things we can touch, smell, see, hear, and taste. This other sense is the feeling of awe when you see a thundering waterfall or spot an animal frolicking in your backyard. It's a sense that tells each and every one of us that we are not alone.

Thousands of societies dwell here on earth. There are insect societies, aquatic societies, animal societies, and societies of divine beings. The society of archangels is just one society of divine beings. Becoming aware that you are a sacred part of each society is the first step to discovering your very own heavenly guides.

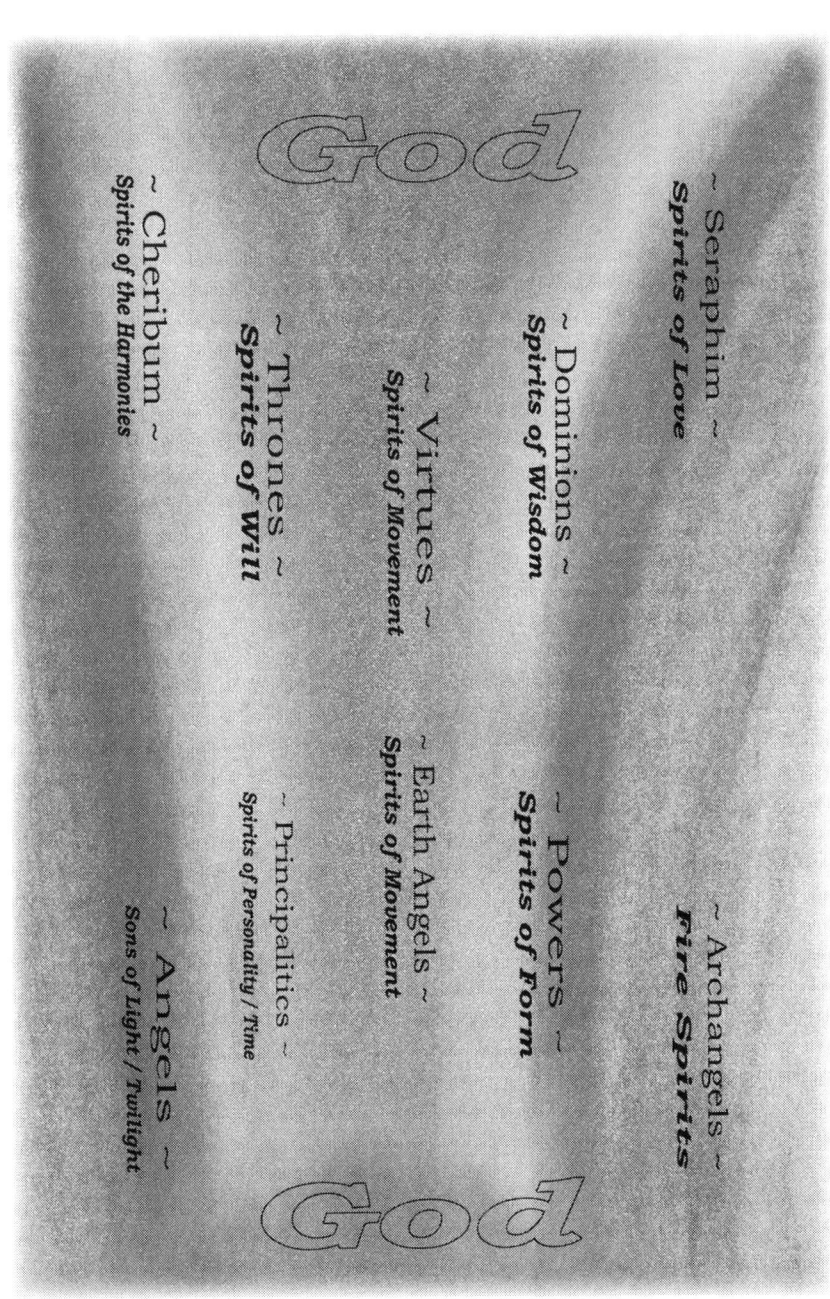

Society of Divine Beings

APPENDIX:

Angel Meditations

Coloring the Angels

SEVEN COLORS OF THE spectrum combine to create pure white light. When combined, the first letter in the name of each of these colors creates the acronym, Roy G. Biv. Remember that name, and you will remember these colors.

Red
Orange
Yellow
Green
Blue
Indigo
Violet

Just like the angels, you have a light inside of you. Called your spirit, this is what connects you to the angel society.

This first simple meditation is a quick, effective way to learn guided breathing. It will help you reunite with your spirit.

In the spirit world, we are all one.

BALLOON BREATHING

Place your right hand on your heart and your left hand on your tummy. Relax and close your eyes.

Take a deep breath. Feel your tummy expand and deflate. As you exhale, imagine you are blowing air into a *red* balloon. See the balloon grow big and round. Let the balloon become so big it is all you can see.

Release the balloon as you inhale.

Watch as the red balloon flies through the air, getting smaller and smaller. Red puffs of air escape and disappear into a mist of brilliant light.

Take another deep breath. Feel your tummy expand and deflate. As you exhale, imagine you are blowing air into an *orange* balloon. See the balloon grow big and round. Let the balloon become so big it is all you can see.

Release the balloon as you inhale.

Watch as the orange balloon flies through the air, getting smaller and smaller. Orange puffs of air escape and disappear into a mist of brilliant light.

Take another deep breath. Feel your tummy expand and deflate. Repeat this breathing exercise imagining a *yellow* balloon, a *green* balloon, a *blue* balloon, an *indigo* balloon, and a *violet* balloon.

When all of the seven colored balloons have been released, look at the empty area that remains. In front of you is a tiny pinpoint of light. That light is the air you released with your balloons.

Breathe slowly and deeply. As you count backward from seven to one, imagine the air from each balloon filling the darkness with its light.

When you reach one, remember your happiest moment. Enjoy the memory. When you are ready, open your eyes.

CALLING ALL ANGELS

Place your right hand on your heart and your left hand on your tummy. Relax and close your eyes. Take a deep breath. Invite the angels to join you.

Exhale. Pure white light radiates all around.

Inhale. A transparent bubble forms around you. Archangel Michael is on your right, Archangel Raphael is on your left, and Archangel Ariel is behind you. Their Band of Mercy stands in the white light. Ask for courage.

Exhale. Darkness forms outside of your bubble. This is fear.

Inhale. The angels boldly raise their shields of white light.

Exhale as your fears melt away.

Inhale pure white light. You are safe inside your bubble.

Exhale. Thank the band of angels for coming.

Breathe in white light as Archangels Chamuel, Jeremiel, and Jophiel enter your bubble. Ask for tenderness.

Exhale. A vast darkness forms outside your bubble. This is hatred.

Inhale. Feel the embrace of your holy guardians. Their love dispels the darkness. You are safe.

Exhale. Thank your guardian angels for coming.

Inhale. Archangels Uriel, Haniel, and Metatron enter your bubble. Ask for wisdom.

Exhale. A grey shadow forms outside your bubble. This is frustration.

Breathe in white light as their choirs of angels lower their brooms and dance around you, gracefully sweeping regret away. You are safe.

Exhale. Thank the angels for coming.

Inhale. Archangels Gabriel, Azrael, and Zadkiel enter your bubble. Ask for confidence.

Exhale. A murky green speck forms outside your bubble. This is doubt.

Inhale as legions of angels reveal your talents. These shining gifts from God dissolve the speck. You are safe.

Exhale. Thank God for your gifts.

Breathe in brilliant colors of light as Archangels Raguel, Sandalphon, and Raziel enter your bubble. As colors fill your bubble, you ask to be one with God.

Exhale all remaining shadows. The angels whisper God's promise. You are love.

Inhale. Fly with the birds in the sky. Swim with the fish in the ocean. Sway with leaves on the trees. Rest with grains of sand.

Exhale. The colors blend into white light. You are the light.

Breathe. When you are ready, open your eyes.

BIBLIOGRAPHY

Bunson, Matthew, **Angels A to Z: Who's Who of the Heavenly Host**, Harmony Publishing, New York, New York, 2004

Dionysius the Areopagite, **The Celestial Hierarchy**, ebook, Kessinger Publishing, Whitefish, Montana, 2010

Holy Bible, King James Version, Oxford University Press, New York

Nyland, Dr. A**, Angels, Archangels and Angel Categories: What the Ancients Said,** Smith and Sterling Publishers, Mermaid Beach, Australia, 2010

Virtue, Doreen, **Archangels and Ascended Masters**, Hay House, Carlsbad, California, 2003

Webster, Richard, **Encyclopedia of Angels**, Llewellyn Publications, Woodbury, Minnesota, 2009

Further Reading

A Course in Miracles, Foundation For Inner Peace, Mill Valley, California, 1975

Dyer, Wayne W., **Wisdom of the Ages**, HarperCollins Publishers, New York, New York, 1998

Hicks, Easter and Jerry, **The Law of Attraction**, Hay House, Carlsbad, California, 2006

Holden, Robert, Ph.D. **Happiness Now,** Hay House, Carlsbad, California, 1998

Jerusalem Bible, Double Day & Company, Garden City, New York, 1996

Lewis, C.S., **The Complete Chronicles of Narnia**, Fontana Lions, 1980

The Book of Enoch, ebook, http://www.munseys.com

Virtue, Doreen, **How to Hear Your Angels**, Hay House, Carlsbad, California, 2007

Williamson, Marianne, **Return to Love**, HarperCollins Publishers, New York, New York, 1992

Printed in Great Britain
by Amazon